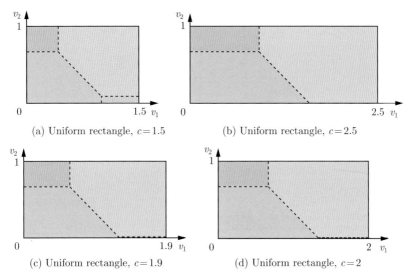

(a) Uniform rectangle, $c=1.5$ (b) Uniform rectangle, $c=2.5$

(c) Uniform rectangle, $c=1.9$ (d) Uniform rectangle, $c=2$

Figure 2.3   Computed solutions vs. optimal solutions for uniform distributions

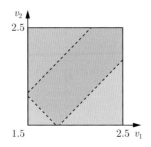

Figure 2.4   Solution comparison in the unit-demand setting

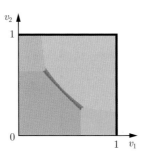

Figure 2.8   The combinatorial value setting

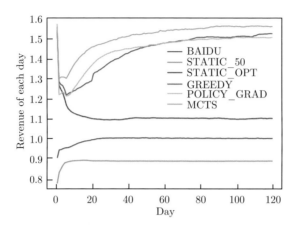

Figure 3.5　Performance of different strategies

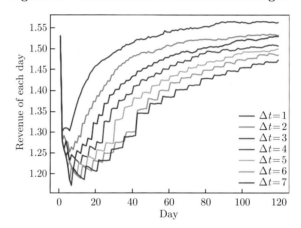

Figure 3.7　Effect of the frequency of changing reserve prices

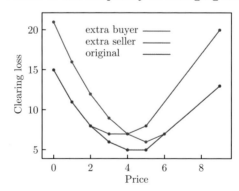

Figure 4.2　Effect on the shape of the clearing loss when adding a

buyer or a seller

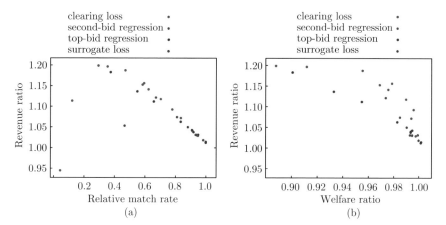

Figure 4.3   Trade-off between revenue improvement and decrease in match rate (a) or buyer welfare (b)

Each point represents the performance of the fitted model under a loss function for a fixed regularization level

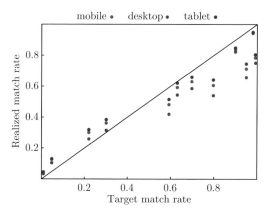

Figure 4.4   Realized match rate against target match rate under the model fit with the clearing loss, broken down by device type

The vertical line denotes the parameter setting $\lambda = 1$ with a target match rate of $1 - 1/e \approx 0.63$

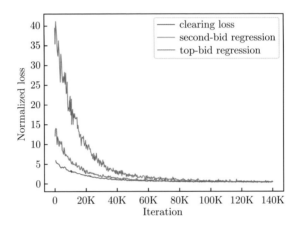

Figure 4.5 Convergence rate of the model under different loss function, in minibatch iterations. We plot the value of each loss across iterations normalized by its value upon convergence

AI-driven
Mechanism Design

人工智能驱动的机制设计 英文版

沈蔚然 唐平中 左 淞 著

清華大學出版社
北京

内 容 简 介

近年来，机制设计在工业界已取得巨大成功。受此影响，机制设计也成为经济学与计算机科学交叉领域的核心研究课题之一。然而，尽管花费数十年的努力，学界在理论与实践方面仍然面临诸多挑战。本书提出了人工智能驱动的机制设计框架，以提供一种替代方法来处理目前机制设计理论与实践中的一些问题。该框架包含两个互相交互的抽象模型：智能体模型和机制模型。结合人工智能与机制设计，我们可以解决利用单一领域技术无法解决的问题。例如极大缩小机制搜索空间、构建更现实的买家模型、更好地平衡各类目标等。本书从多物品拍卖，动态拍卖，以及多目标拍卖三个场景入手，分析并说明该框架对理论与实践均有帮助。

本书可供从事人工智能驱动设计及相关领域的高校师生、研究人员及相关技术人员阅读参考。

图书在版编目（CIP）数据

人工智能驱动的机制设计：英文/沈蔚然，唐平中，左淞著.—北京：清华大学出版社，2023.8
ISBN 978-7-302-63283-2

Ⅰ.①人…　Ⅱ.①沈…②唐…③左…　Ⅲ.①人工智能-应用-机制设计理论-英文
Ⅳ.①F062.5-39

中国国家版本馆 CIP 数据核字（2023）第 059400 号

责任编辑：孙亚楠
封面设计：常雪影
责任校对：赵丽敏
责任印制：杨　艳

出版发行：清华大学出版社
　　　　　网　　址：http://www.tup.com.cn，http://www.wqbook.com
　　　　　地　　址：北京清华大学学研大厦 A 座　　　邮　　编：100084
　　　　　社 总 机：010-83470000　　　　　　　　　邮　　购：010-62786544
　　　　　投稿与读者服务：010-62776969，c-service@tup.tsinghua.edu.cn
　　　　　质量反馈：010-62772015，zhiliang@tup.tsinghua.edu.cn
印 装 者：天津鑫丰华印务有限公司
经　　销：全国新华书店
开　　本：155mm×235mm　　　印　张：10.25　　插　页：2　　字　数：184 千字
版　　次：2023 年 10 月第 1 版　　　　　　　印　次：2023 年 10 月第 1 次印刷
定　　价：79.00 元

产品编号：092071-01

Preface

In recent decades, the area of mechanism design has undergone remarkable advancements. Among all its applications, online ad auctions stand out as one of the most important industries deeply rooted in mechanism design theory. These auctions have become a major revenue source for Internet giants like Google, Amazon, Alibaba, and Facebook.

Despite the huge success of mechanism design, a large gap persists between theory and practice. Take, for instance, the design of auction rules. While we have a clear understanding of revenue-maximizing mechanisms for simple scenarios, such as selling a single item, the problem becomes very challenging when multiple items are involved due to the vast design space. Furthermore, mechanism design theory often operates under the assumption that all buyers are fully rational actors and have access to enough information and computational power to figure out the optimal strategy. This draws a sharp contrast to the diverse goals and irrational behaviors of real-world buyers. Besides, online ad auction platforms possess a large amount of bidding data that the conventional mechanism design theory overlooks, data that could revolutionize the way of designing auctions optimized for real-world performance.

This book emerges as a bridge over these gaps, uniting mechanism design theory with the powerful tools of artificial intelligence. This fusion harnesses the flexibility of AI techniques to manage vast datasets while preserving the economic properties from theoretical analyses. We aim to demonstrate the multifaceted applications of AI techniques in the domain of mechanism design. We hope this perspective will offer both researchers and practitioners a fresh point of view for studying these intricate problems.

Moreover, we explore how computer science and economics can

mutually enrich each other, promoting interdisciplinary collaboration. The union of these disciplines not only addresses the deficiencies in current theory but also opens up new possibilities for research and application.

Contents

Chapter 1 Introduction ·· 1

  1.1 Mechanism Design ·· 2

      1.1.1 Social Choice Function ······························· 2

      1.1.2 Mechanism ·· 2

      1.1.3 Implementation ······································· 3

      1.1.4 Revelation Principle ·································· 4

      1.1.5 Efficient Mechanisms ································· 5

  1.2 Auctions ·· 7

  1.3 Why AI-Driven ·· 11

      1.3.1 Challenges in Auction Design ······················ 11

      1.3.2 The AI-Driven Framework ·························· 12

  1.4 Organization of the Book ··································· 13

  References ··· 14

Chapter 2 Multi-Dimensional Mechanism Design via AI-Driven Approaches ·································· 16

  2.1 Recovering Optimal Mechanisms with Simple Neural Networks ·· 16

      2.1.1 Background ··· 17

      2.1.2 Setting ·· 19

      2.1.3 Revisiting the Naïve Mechanism ··················· 21

      2.1.4 Network Structure of MENUNET ··················· 24

      2.1.5 Recovering Known Results ·························· 27

2.2 Discovering Unknown Optimal Mechanisms · · · · · · · · · · · · · ·30

   2.2.1 Experiment Results ·31

   2.2.2 Theoretic Analysis and Formal Proofs · · · · · · · · · · · ·34

2.3 Performance ·52

References ·56

Chapter 3 Dynamic Mechanism Design via AI-Driven

          Approaches ·59

3.1 Dynamic Cost-Per-Action Auctions with Ex-Post IR

   Guarantees ·60

   3.1.1 Background ·60

   3.1.2 Our Contributions ·62

   3.1.3 Related Works ·63

   3.1.4 Setting and Preliminaries ·64

   3.1.5 Mechanisms ·70

   3.1.6 Truthfulness and Implementation · · · · · · · · · · · · · · ·74

   3.1.7 Impossibility Result ·80

3.2 Dynamic Reserve Pricing via Reinforcement Mechanism

   Design ·80

   3.2.1 Background ·81

   3.2.2 Settings and Preliminaries ·86

   3.2.3 Bidder Behavior Model ·88

   3.2.4 Dynamic Mechanism Design as Markov Decision

       Process ·93

References ·103

Chapter 4 Multi-Objective Mechanism Design via

          AI-Driven Approaches ·109

4.1 Balancing Objectives through Approximation Analysis · · ·110

   4.1.1 Background ·110

   4.1.2 Settings and Preliminaries ·113

        4.1.3   Generalized Virtual-Efficient Mechanisms · · · · · · · · · 114

        4.1.4   Experiments · 126

    4.2   Balancing Objectives through Machine Learning · · · · · · · · · 128

        4.2.1   Background · 129

        4.2.2   Market Clearing Loss · 132

        4.2.3   Theoretical Guarantees · 138

        4.2.4   Empirical Evaluation · 140

    References · 146

Chapter 5   Summary and Future Directions · · · · · · · · · · · · · · · · · 151

    References · 153

Chapter 1   Introduction

Mechanism design has become one of the most important research topics in economics in the past few decades. Recently, it has also been intensively studied in computer science, due to its successful applications in the online advertising industry. In 2018, the world's largest search engine, Google LLC., generated \$116.3 billion's revenue through online advertising[1]. And the largest Chinese search engine Baidu also had annual revenue of \$11.9 billion from its PC and mobile advertising platforms[2].

Companies like Google and Baidu sell ads through their search engines (sponsored search auctions) and ad exchanges. When a user searches a keyword in a search engine, several ads are displayed before the algorithmic results. The space that contains the ads is called *slots*. In ad exchanges, publishers submit their available slots to the exchange and the exchange sells them to the advertisers. Both search engines and ad exchanges sell these slots through auctions, where mechanism design plays a key role in defining auction rules.

This chapter first introduces the general mechanism design setting and how it is related to auctions. Then, we discuss some challenges in both mechanism design theory and application, and also the gap between them. In the end, we present a general framework, which we call the AI-driven mechanism design framework, and explain briefly how this framework can be applied to different types of mechanism design problems.

1.1　Mechanism Design

Mechanism design is also called "reverse game theory". Its goal is to design game rules to incentivize rational players to behave in a desirable way. In this section, we briefly discuss the mechanism design theory, and introduce some definitions and classic results that are intensively used throughout the entire book.

1.1.1　Social Choice Function

The goal of the mechanism designer is to induce the desired outcome, in an environment where the agents are strategic. An outcome can be an allocation of a certain resource or a place for building a public facility. Let O be the set of all possible outcomes. Denote by N the set of all agents and assume $|N| = n$. Each agent has his own preference $\succ_i$ over different outcomes. For example, $O \succ_i O'$ means agent i prefers outcome O over O'. Let $\succ = (\succ_1, \succ_2, \cdots, \succ_n)$ be the preference profile of the agents, and P be the set of all possible preference profiles. Given the preference profile of all agents, a *social choice* function chooses an outcome from the set O.

Definition 1.1 (Social choice function) A social choice function C is a function that maps P to O: $C : P \mapsto O$.

A *utility function* $u_i : O \mapsto \mathbb{R}$ is also widely used to describe an agent's preference. When utility functions are used, a social choice function becomes $C : U \mapsto O$, where U is the set of all possible utility function profiles.

It is possible that sometimes a social choice function may return multiple possible outcomes with a corresponding probability distribution.

1.1.2　Mechanism

A mechanism collects the agents' reported utility function profile (not necessarily equal to the true utility function profile u), and outputs an outcome. However, mechanism design is usually considered in Bayesian settings[3], where each agent i has a private type θ_i that determines his utility function. It is often assumed that the type profile

$\theta = (\theta_1, \theta_2, \cdots, \theta_n)$ is drawn from a publicly known joint distribution $f(\theta)$, but θ_i is only known to agent i after it is realized.

Definition 1.2 A Bayesian game setting is a tuple (N, O, Θ, f, u), where:

- N is a set of agents;
- O is a set of outcomes;
- $\Theta = \Theta_1 \times \Theta_2 \times \cdots \times \Theta_n$ is a set of possible type profiles;
- $f : \Theta \mapsto \mathbb{R}_+$ is a probability distribution over Θ;
- $u : \Theta \times O \mapsto \mathbb{R}^n$ is the agents' utility function profile.

With such a Bayesian game setting, a mechanism can be defined as follows:

Definition 1.3 (Mechanism) A mechanism, with respect to a Bayesian game setting (N, O, Θ, f, u), is a tuple (A, M) where:

- $A = A_1 \times A_2 \times \cdots \times A_n$ is the set of possible action profiles;
- $M : A \mapsto O$ selects an outcome according to the agents' actions.

Once a mechanism is announced to the agents, a Bayesian game is naturally induced, where agent i's action set is A_i, and his expected utility function $u_i : \Theta_i \times A \mapsto \mathbb{R}$ is

$$u_i(\theta_i, a) = \mathrm{E}_{\theta_{-i}}\left[u_i(\theta, M(a))\right]$$

where $a \in A$ is the action profile, $\theta_{-i} = (\theta_1, \cdots, \theta_{i-1}, \theta_{i+1}, \cdots, \theta_n)$ is the type profile of all agents except i. And if each agent uses a mixed strategy s_i, then the utility function becomes

$$u_i(\theta_i, s) = \sum_{a \in A} s(a)\, \mathrm{E}_{\theta_{-i}}\left[u_i(\theta, M(a))\right]$$

where $s(a)$ is the probability that action profile a occurs in strategy profile s.

1.1.3 Implementation

Now we consider the agents' strategic behaviors. Given a mechanism (A, M), in its induced Bayesian game, the agents' strategies form a Bayes-Nash equilibrium[1], i.e., each agent chooses the strategy s_i^* that maximizes his utility:

---

[1] Throughout this book, we always assume that such a Bayes-Nash equilibrium exists.

$$s_i^* = \arg\max_{s_i} u_i(\theta_i, s) = \arg\max_{s_i} \sum_{a \in A} s(a) \mathrm{E}_{\theta_{-i}} \left[u_i(\theta, M(a)) \right]$$

It is clear that the outcome of the mechanism depends on the agents' actions, which in turn depends on their types. Thus every mechanism (A, M) actually implements a certain social choice function.

However, not every social choice function is implementable. Due to the agents' strategic behaviors, they may choose actions to benefit themselves, which could prevent certain outcomes from happening. To study implementable social choice functions, we have the following definition:

Definition 1.4 (Implementation in Bayes-Nash equilibrium) A mechanism (A, M) is an implementation of a social choice function C in Bayes-Nash equilibrium, if there is a *Bayes-Nash equilibrium* in the induced Bayesian game, and for every type profile θ, for every possible action profile a^* in the Bayes-Nash equilibrium given θ, $M(a^*) = C(u^\theta)$, where $u^\theta(a) = u(\theta, a)$ is the true utility function profile of the agents.

Similarly, if the induced game has a dominant strategy equilibrium, then we can have a stronger notion of implementation.

Definition 1.5 (Implementation in dominant strategies) A mechanism (A, M) is an implementation of a social choice function C in dominant strategies, if there is a *dominant strategies equilibrium* in the induced Bayesian game, and for the equilibrium action profile a^*, $M(a^*) = C(u^\theta)$, where $u^\theta(a) = u(\theta, a)$ is the true utility function profile of the agents.

1.1.4 Revelation Principle

In the above discussion, each agent's type set Θ_i may not be the same as his action set A_i. We call such mechanisms *indirect mechanisms*. Similarly, if for each agent i, his action is to report his type directly to the mechanism, i.e., $\Theta_i = A_i$, such mechanisms are called *direct mechanisms*. An issue with direct mechanisms is that the agents may have incentives to lie about their types.

Definition 1.6 (Incentive compatibility (IC), truthfulness) A direct mechanism is *dominant-strategy incentive compatible*, or *dominant-strategy truthful*, if for each agent, reporting his true type is always the best action, regardless of other agents' types, i.e.,

$$\theta_i = \arg\max_{\theta'_i \in \Theta_i} u_i(\theta, M(\theta'_i, \theta_{-i})), \forall \theta_i, \theta'_i, \theta_{-i}, \forall i \in N$$

Similarly, a direct mechanism is *Bayesian incentive compatible*, if for each agent, reporting his true type maximizes his expected utility:

$$\theta_i = \arg\max_{\theta'_i \in \Theta_i} \mathrm{E}_{\theta_{-i}}\left[u_i(\theta, M(\theta'_i, \theta_{-i}))\right], \forall \theta_i, \theta'_i, \forall i \in N$$

At first glance, it seems that indirect mechanisms can implement a larger set of social choice functions than direct ones, as direct mechanisms pose additional constraints on the action sets. Furthermore, direct mechanisms may not be truthful, and thus may not be able to select certain outcomes if the agents have incentives to misreport their types.

However, the following *revelation principle*[4] shows that truthful direct mechanisms have the same power as indirect mechanisms in terms of implementable social choice functions.

Theorem 1.1 (Revelation principle) *If a social choice function C can be implemented by an indirect mechanism in dominant strategies (Bayes-Nash equilibrium), then it can also be implemented by a truthful direct mechanism in dominant strategies (Bayes-Nash equilibrium).*

According to Theorem 1.1, truthful direct mechanisms and indirect mechanisms can implement the same set of social choice functions. Therefore, it is without loss of generality to only focus on truthful direct mechanisms.

1.1.5   Efficient Mechanisms

In some applications, we allow monetary transfers among the agents and the mechanism designer. For example, when a seller sells an item to many buyers, the mechanism designer needs to determine who gets the item and how much each buyer should pay to the seller. In such cases, the outcome of a mechanism consists of both an allocation x and a payment p. Let $u_i(x, p; \theta_i)$ be the utility function of agent i if the outcome is (x, p). A standard assumption in the literature is to assume that each agent's utility function is quasi-linear:

$$u_i(x, p; \theta_i) = v_i(x; \theta_i) - p_i$$

where $v_i(x; \theta_i)$ measures how the agent values the allocation and p_i is the amount of money this agent has to pay to the mechanism. An important goal of mechanism designers in the quasi-linear setting is to ensure that each agent does not lose by participating in the mechanism.

Definition 1.7 (Individual rationality (IR)) A mechanism in the quasi-linear setting is said to be *ex-post* individually rational, if each agent's utility is always non-negative, regardless of other agents' type profile, i.e.,

$$u_i(x(\theta), p(\theta); \theta_i) \geqslant 0, \forall \theta \in \Theta, \forall i \in N$$

A mechanism in the quasi-linear setting is said to be *interim* individually rational, if each agent's expected utility after realizing his type is non-negative:

$$\mathrm{E}_{\theta_{-i}}\left[u_i(x(\theta_i, \theta_{-i}), p(\theta_i, \theta_{-i}); \theta_i)\right] \geqslant 0, \forall \theta_i, \forall i \in N$$

Similarly, a mechanism is said to be *ex-ante* individually rational, if each agent's expected utility before realizing his type is non-negative:

$$\mathrm{E}_\theta\left[u_i(x(\theta), p(\theta); \theta_i)\right] \geqslant 0, \forall i \in N$$

Since the mechanism charges the agents, we can define the *revenue* of the mechanism as the total payments from the agents.

Definition 1.8 (Revenue) The expected revenue of a mechanism $M = (x, p)$ is

$$\mathrm{REV}(x, p) = \mathrm{E}_\theta\left[\sum_{i \in N} p_i(\theta)\right]$$

We also define the *social welfare* of a mechanism as follows:

Definition 1.9 (Social welfare) The social welfare of a mechanism $M = (x, p)$ is

$$\mathrm{WEL}(x, p) = \mathrm{E}_\theta\left[\sum_{i \in N} v_i(x(\theta); \theta_i)\right]$$

A mechanism is said to be *efficient* if it maximizes the social welfare. A well-known class of efficient mechanisms is the *Groves mechanisms*.

Definition 1.10 (Groves mechanisms) The Groves mechanisms is a class of mechanisms (x, p) where:

$$\begin{cases} x(\theta) = \arg\max_x \sum_{i \in N} v_i(x(\theta); \theta_i) \\ p_i(\theta) = c_i(\theta_{-i}) - \sum_{j \neq i} v_j(x(\theta); \theta_j) \end{cases}$$

where $c_i(\theta_{-i})$ is a function that does not depend on θ_i.

One nice property of the Groves mechanisms is that any such mechanism is dominant strategy incentive compatible.   The utility function of each agent is

$$u_i(x(\theta), p(\theta); \theta_i) = v_i(x(\theta); \theta_i) - p_i(\theta)$$

$$= \left[\sum_{j \in N} v_j(x(\theta); \theta_j) \right] - c_i(\theta_{-i})$$

Note that the second term does not depend on θ_i. Thus if agent i tries to maximize his utility, he is actually maximizing the first term, which is the same as the goal of the mechanism. Therefore, such mechanisms ensure that externalities are internalized.

Particularly, we can set

$$c_i(\theta_{-i}) = \sum_{j \neq i} v_j(x(\theta_{-i}); \theta_j)$$

This mechanism is called the *Vickrey-Clarke-Groves mechanism* (VCG).

Definition 1.11 (Vickrey-Clarke-Groves mechanism) The VCG mechanism is defined as follows:

$$x(\theta) = \arg\max_x \sum_{i \in N} v_i(x(\theta); \theta_i),$$

$$p_i(\theta) = \sum_{j \neq i} v_j(x(\theta_{-i}); \theta_j) - \sum_{j \neq i} v_j(x(\theta); \theta_j)$$

1.2   Auctions

In this section, we discuss a special protocol of allocating items to a number of agents called auctions. In a general m-item auction, there are n buyers and a seller who has m items for sale. Let M and N be the set of items and the set of buyers, respectively. Each buyer's type is his valuation function over obtained items (fractional units can be viewed as the probability of obtaining an item) $v_i : [0,1]^m \mapsto \mathbb{R}_+$. Let V be the set of all possible valuation function profiles v. Similar to the general mechanism design setting discussed in Section 1.1, an auction mechanism (x, p) consists of an allocation function $x(v)$ and a payment function $p(v)$, where

- $x_i : V \mapsto [0,1]^m$ specifies how many units of each item should be allocated to buyer i;
- $p_i : V \mapsto \mathbb{R}_+$ is the amount of money that buyer i should pay to the mechanism.

$x_i(v)$ and $p_i(v)$ are also referred to as *ex-post* rules. Let $x_{i,j}$ be the j-th element of x_i, or equivalently the allocation of item j to buyer i. If $0 < x_{i,j} < 1$, we say that item j is allocated to buyer i with probability $x_{i,j}$. And if $x_{i,j} \in \{0,1\}$, for all $i \in N$ and $j \in M$ we say that the mechanism is *deterministic*.

Of course, with the above definitions, each mechanism should satisfy some feasibility constraints to guarantee that no more than 1 unit of each item will ever be allocated.

$$\sum_{i=1}^{n} x_{i,j} \leqslant 1, \forall j \in M$$

In particular, the buyers' utility functions are often assumed to be additive, quasi-linear, and have no externalities. In this case, a buyer's type can be simply represented by an m-dimensional vector $v_i \in \mathbb{R}_+^m$, with each element being the value for the corresponding item. Each buyer's value v_i is drawn from a joint distribution $f_i(v_i)$ that is publicly known. Thus, the utility of buyer i is

$$u_i(x_i(v), p_i(v)) = \sum_{j=1}^{m} v_{i,j} x_{i,j}(v) - p_i(v) \qquad (1.1)$$

where $v_{i,j}$ is the buyer i's value for item j.

Similarly, we can also define the social welfare and revenue of an auction:

$$\mathrm{WEL}(x,p) = \mathrm{E}_v \left[\sum_{i=1}^{n} \sum_{j=1}^{m} v_{i,j} x_{i,j}(v) \right],$$

$$\mathrm{REV}(x,p) = \mathrm{E}_v \left[\sum_{i=1}^{n} p_i(v) \right]$$

The VCG mechanism also applies here and it still maximizes the social welfare, i.e., the VCG mechanism is an efficient auction mechanism. Optimizing revenue, however, is a much more challenging task, and only some special cases have been solved so far.

Designing revenue maximizing auctions has been one of the most important research agendas. The seminal work by Myerson[4] solves the problem of how to sell one item optimally. However, the optimal mechanism for selling multiple items still remains largely unknown after decades of research efforts, except for some special cases. Therefore, in this section, we mainly focus on the single-item auction setting, i.e., $m = 1$. In this setting, the allocation function becomes a scalar function.

Before we consider the optimal auction, let's first characterize the set of all truthful mechanisms. According to the revelation principle (Theorem 1.1), it is without loss of generality to consider only truthful direct mechanisms. A natural question to ask is how to ensure the truthfulness of a direct mechanism. To answer this question, we first define the following interim rules.

Definition 1.12 (Interim allocation and payment) The interim allocation rule and payment rule with respect to a mechanism (x,p) are

$$x_i(v_i) = \mathrm{E}_{v_{-i}} \left[x_i(v_i, v_{-i}) \right], \forall v_i, \forall i \in N,$$

$$p_i(v_i) = \mathrm{E}_{v_{-i}} \left[p_i(v_i, v_{-i}) \right], \forall v_i, \forall i \in N$$

Note that we abuse notation in the above definition and employ x_i and p_i to represent both interim and ex-post rules. There is no ambiguity since the interim rules only take a scalar as input.

Using the above definition, Myerson[4] provides the following characterization of truthful mechanisms.

Lemma 1.1 (Myerson's Lemma) *An auction mechanism (x,p) is Bayesian incentive compatible, if and only if*

- *The interim allocation rule $x_i(v_i)$ is monotone increasing in v_i;*
- *The interim payment rule $p_i(v_i)$ satisfies:*

$$p_i(v_i) = p_i(0) + \int_0^{v_i} s \, dx_i(s), \forall i \in N$$

The two conditions in the above lemma are often referred to as *allocation monotonicity* and *payment identity*, respectively. With Lemma 1.1, we only need to focus on mechanisms that satisfy these two conditions. Clearly, in order to maximize revenue while at the same time guarantee IR, we need to set $p_i(0) = 0$.

To study the mechanism that maximizes the revenue, we first define the *virtual value function*, which also follows Myerson[4].

Definition 1.13 (Virtual value) Let $F_i(v_i)$ be the cumulative value distribution of buyer i, and assume that $F_i(v_i)$ is differentiable (i.e., the density function $f_i(v_i)$ exists). The virtual value of buyer i with value v_i is

$$\varphi_i(v_i) = v_i - \frac{1 - F_i(v_i)}{f_i(v_i)}$$

A virtual value function is said to be regular, if $\varphi_i(v_i)$ is monotone increasing in v_i.

We make the standard assumption that the virtual value function for each buyer is *regular*. Myerson[4] also shows that the revenue of a mechanism (x, p) can be expressed in terms of virtual values.

Lemma 1.2 *The revenue of a truthful mechanism (x, p) is*

$$\text{REV}(x, p) = E_v \left[\sum_{i=1}^n p_i(v) \right] = E_v \left[\sum_{i=1}^n x_i(v_i) \varphi_i(v_i) \right]$$

According to Lemma 1.2, to optimize the revenue, we should always maximize the sum of virtual values. And of course, if all buyers have negative virtual values, then no one wins the item. In the regular case, this is equivalent to setting a *reserve price* r_i for each buyer such that

$$\varphi_i(r_i) = 0$$

Therefore, the optimal auction allocates the item to the buyer with the highest virtual value among those whose bids are higher than their respective reserve prices.

1.3   Why AI-Driven

There is still a huge gap between the theory and application of auction design, despite decades of efforts. In this section, we first discuss some challenges in auction design. Then we propose the AI-driven framework, aiming to provide an alternative method to bridge the gap.

1.3.1   Challenges in Auction Design

Myerson[4] gave the revenue optimal auction for selling a single item in his seminal work. Since then, theories have been developed to generalize the setting to the so-called *single parameter setting*[5-6], where each buyer's utility function can be fully characterized by a single parameter. However, after decades of efforts, our understanding of how to sell multiple items optimally still remains largely unknown, even in the case of a single buyer, except for some specific cases[7-10]. Such challenges in theoretical analysis motivate another way of analyzing the multi-item auction problem[11-13], by applying techniques from algorithm design to find near-optimal solutions instead. There is also another line of work called the automated mechanism design, that incorporates AI approaches[14-15], such as modeling the problem as a constraint satisfaction problem. However, most of these approaches only produce mechanisms that are approximately optimal or truthful. Furthermore, they also suffer from heavy computational burdens.

Another major challenge in auction design is its application. The dominating and standard auction mechanism in the online advertising industry is the so-called *generalized second price auction (GSP)*[16-17], which is neither truthful nor optimal. Standard auction design theory is developed based on a number of unrealistic assumptions. For example, the buyers are assumed to be rational and bid according to some equilibrium of the induced game. But it is not clear why the buyers have all the necessary information and computational power to compute such an equilibrium before placing bids. In contrast to the single parameter setting, buyers can have multi-dimensional utilities and complex preferences in reality. But standard mechanism design theory assumes that the buyers have additive and quasi-linear utilities. Moreover, many theoretical studies focus on one-shot auctions, while many real auction applications, such as the online advertising platforms, auctions are run in a repeated fashion, where the buyers' behaviors can be much more complex and the mechanism design space is significantly larger. Also, most advertising platforms focus on multiple objectives rather than a single one. Thus they are interested in designing mechanisms that have good performance in multiple aspects. Such gaps pose a serious challenge in putting auction theory into practice.

1.3.2   The AI-Driven Framework

We propose the AI-driven mechanism design framework, aiming to provide an alternative way of dealing with these challenges (see Figure 1.1).

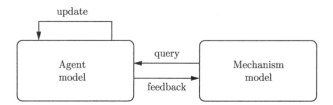

Figure 1.1   The AI-driven mechanism design framework

The AI-driven mechanism design framework has two abstract models: the agent model and the mechanism model. These two models interact with each other and we are able to optimize or update the mechanism through the interactions.

The agent model describes how the agents behave. It can be the standard rational model as often assumed in the literature, or a machine learning model learned from real data. For example, Section 3.2 uses a recurrent neural network (RNN) that takes into consideration the buyers' performance statistics such as the number of impressions and clicks; Section 4.1 adopts the standard rational model; Chapter 2 allows any agent model that can be represented by a neural network.

The mechanism model consists of both a mechanism described by parameters or states, and an optimization algorithm or any AI approach to update and improve the mechanism. The mechanism model queries the agent model with its current parameters or state and obtains the agents' reactions as feedback. And according to the feedback, the mechanism can be optimized or improved using AI approaches. The mechanism model can be tailored specifically to fit the agent model. For example, it can be an automated mechanism design (AMD) [15, 18], a reinforcement mechanism design (RMD) (see Section 3.2), or even a neural network that optimizes certain parameters of the auction (see Section 3.2 and 4.2).

1.4   Organization of the Book

Chapter 2 shows how the AI-driven mechanism design framework can be applied to multi-dimensional mechanism design. We focus on the theoretical analysis of the multi-item single buyer case. Both the buyer and the mechanism are represented by neural networks. We make use of the menu interpretation to significantly simplify the networks. We implement the framework in a number of settings, and show that the framework not only reproduces some known results but can also help us derive unknown results in terms of designing optimal mechanisms in complex settings.

Chapter 3 describes how this framework can be applied to dynamic mechanism design problems that arise from real world sponsored search auction platforms. We focus on two concrete settings. In the first setting, we propose an RNN-based Markov buyer behavior model and fit the model using real data from Baidu, the major Chinese search engine. We then formulate the dynamic mechanism design problem as a Markov decision process (MDP) and solve the MDP using reinforcement learning techniques. This framework has been adopted by Baidu and was highlighted in its 2018 Q1 Financial Reports [2]. In the second setting, we focus on the ex-post IR cost-per-action (advertisers pay only when users make purchases) auction mechanisms, instead of the current standard cost-per-click (advertisers pay when users click-through the ads) model.

In such a setting, the buyers require ex-post IR guarantees, which is one major reason that motivates this study. We provide a "credit" solution to this problem. We also show that there is no non-trivial mechanism that is both dynamic IC and ex-post IR. Therefore, a stronger notion of IR comes at the cost of a weaker notion of IC.

Chapter 4 shows how to design mechanisms to tradeoff between different objectives using the AI-driven mechanism design framework. In Section 4.1, we propose a class of mechanisms with a simple parameter. We show that, simply by tuning the parameter, one can easily obtain different tradeoff results, and at the same time guarantee to have a near-optimal revenue. In Section 4.2, we use machine learning approaches to learn a pricing policy for auctions with context information. We come up with a new loss function that is convex and has a simple interpretation. Our experiments show that our approach outperforms previous ones in terms of balancing different objectives.

Chapter 5 summarizes the book and discusses possible future research directions.

References

[1] Alphabet Inc. Alphabet investor relations. https://abc.xyz/investor/, 2018. Accessed: 2019-03-26.

[2] Baidu Inc. Baidu Inc., first quarter 2018 financial reports [R/OL]. http://ir.baidu.com/static-files/626b8f84-5d34-49b7-b4ab-4f9f03cb8a2b.

[3] SHOHAM Y, LEYTON-BROWN K. Multiagent systems: Algorithmic, game-theoretic, and logical foundations[M]. Cambridge University Press, 2008.

[4] MYERSON R B. Optimal auction design[J]. Mathematics of Operations Research, 1981, 6(1):58–73.

[5] NISAN N, ROUGHGARDEN T, TARDOS E, et al. Algorithmic Game Theory[M]. Cambridge University Press, New York, NY, USA, 2007.

[6] MASKIN E, RILEY J, HAHN F. Optimal multi-unit auctions[J]. The Economics of Missing Markets, Information, and Games, 1989.

[7] ARMSTRONG M. Multiproduct nonlinear pricing[J]. Econometrica, 1996, 64(1):51.

[8] PAVLOV G. Optimal mechanism for selling two goods[J]. The BE Journal of Theoretical Economics, 2011, 11(1).

[9] TANG P, WANG Z. Optimal mechanisms with simple menus[J]. Journal of Mathematical Economics, 2017.

[10] DASKALAKIS C. Multi-item auctions defying intuition?[J]. ACM SIGecom Exchanges, 2015, 14(1): 41–75.

[11] CAI Y, DASKALAKIS C, WEINBERG S M. An algorithmic characterization of multi-dimensional mechanisms[C]//Proceedings of the Forty-Fourth annual ACM symposium on Theory of Computing. ACM, 2012: 459–478.

[12] ALAEI S, FU H, HAGHPANAH N, et al. Bayesian optimal auctions via multi-to single-agent reduction[C]//Proceedings of the 13th ACM Conference on Electronic Commerce. ACM, 2012: 17.

[13] HART S, NISAN N. Approximate revenue maximization with multiple items[J]. Journal of Economic Theory, 2017, 172:313–347.

[14] CONITZER V, SANDHOLM T. Complexity of mechanism design[C]// Proceedings of the Eighteenth Conference on Uncertainty in Artificial Intelligence. Morgan Kaufmann Publishers Inc., 2002: 103–110.

[15] SANDHOLM T, LIKHODEDOV A. Automated design of revenue-maximizing combinatorial auctions[J]. Operations Research, 2015, 63(5):1000–1025.

[16] EDELMAN B, OSTROVSKY M, SCHWARZ M. Internet advertising and the generalized second-price auction: Selling billions of dollars worth of keywords[J]. The American Economic Review, 2007, 97(1):242–259.

[17] VARIAN H R. Position auctions[J]. International Journal of Industrial Organization, 2007, 25(6):1163–1178.

[18] CONITZER V, SANDHOLM T. Automated mechanism design for a self-interested designer[C]//Proceedings of the 4th ACM Conference on Electronic Commerce. ACM, 2003: 232–233.

Chapter 2   Multi-Dimensional Mechanism Design via AI-Driven Approaches[①]

This chapter describes how the AI-driven mechanism design framework can be used to help us discover theoretical results. In Section 2.1, we use our framework to recover known results and compare with analytic solutions, demonstrating its ability in obtaining the optimal mechanism. In Section 2.2, we apply our framework in settings where the optimal mechanisms are unknown before. With the help of our framework, we are able to prove that the mechanisms found by the framework are indeed optimal. To the best of our knowledge, our method is the first to apply neural networks to discover optimal auction mechanisms with provable optimality.

2.1   Recovering Optimal Mechanisms with Simple Neural Networks

As mentioned in Section 1.3, revenue optimal auctions in multi-item settings are still largely unknown. Previous approaches that attempt to design revenue optimal auctions for the multi-item settings fall short in at least one of the three aspects:

- Representation: search in a space that may not even contain the optimal mechanism;

---

① This chapter was originally published as reference [1]: Weiran Shen, Pingzhong Tang, and Song Zuo.   Automated mechanism design via neural networks[C]//Proceedings of the 18th International Conference on Autonomous Agents and Multiagent Systems. AAMAS, 2019: 215-223.

- Strictness: find a mechanism that may not be truthful or optimal;
- Domain dependence: need different designs for different auction settings.

To tackle these difficulties, we apply the AI-driven mechanism design framework and obtain a unified neural network-based framework, which we call MENUNET, that automatically learns to design revenue optimal mechanisms. The framework consists of a mechanism network that produces a mechanism, as well as a buyer network that takes a mechanism as input and gives the actions as output. Such a separation in design mitigates the difficulty to impose incentive compatibility constraints on the mechanism, by making it a rational choice of the buyer. As a result, our framework easily overcomes the previously mentioned difficulties in incorporating incentive-compatibility constraints and always produces strictly incentive compatible mechanisms.

In this section, we implement the neural network in a number of multi-item auction design settings, where the optimal mechanisms are already known. As stated in Section 1.3, only very specific auction settings have known optimal mechanisms. The aim of this section is to show the ability of our neural network in finding optimal mechanisms by comparing with known ones.

2.1.1   Background

Designing optimal mechanisms for selling multiple items has been established as an important research agenda at the interface of economics and computer sciences [2-12].

Due to the diversity in the researchers' backgrounds, there are a number of different angles to study this problem. The standard economics theme aims to understand the optimal mechanisms in various settings. To name a few, Armstrong[13] obtains the revenue optimal mechanisms of selling two items to one buyer, whose valuations of the two items are perfectly positively correlated (a ray through the origin). Manelli and Vincent[14] obtain a partial characterization of optimal mechanisms, in the form of extreme points in the machinery spaces. Pavlov[15] derives optimal mechanisms for two items when the buyer has symmetric uniform distributions. Daskalakis et al.[16] characterize sufficient and necessary conditions for a mechanism to be optimal and derive optimal mechanisms for selling two items for several valuation distributions. Tang and Wang[12] obtain the revenue optimal mechanisms for selling two items, where the valuations are negatively correlated. Yao[10] obtains the revenue optimal mechanisms of selling two additive items to multiple buyers, whose valuations towards the items are binary and independent.

Another category of research rooted in the algorithmic game theory community aims to resolve the difficulties of characterizing optimal mechanisms via the lens of algorithm design. Cai et al.[5] and Alaei et al.[17] give algorithmic characterizations of the optimal Bayesian incentive compatible mechanisms on discrete distributions using linear programs. Hart and Nisan[4], Hartline and Roughgarden[3], Yao[8] provide approximately optimal mechanisms in various settings. Carroll[18] shows that for a certain multi-dimensional screening problem, the worst-case optimal mechanism is simply to sell each item separately.

The third category is closely related to the AI-driven mechanism design framework. These works aim to search for optimal mechanisms via various AI approaches. Conitzer and Sandholm[2] model the problem of revenue and welfare maximization as an instance of the constraint satisfaction problem (CSP) through which the optimal mechanism may be found using various searching techniques, despite its general computational complexity. Sandholm and Likhodedov[9] model a restricted revenue maximization problem (within affine maximizing auctions) as a parameter searching problem in a multi-dimensional parameter space, and they find several sets of parameters that yield good empirical revenue. Dütting et al.[19] aim to learn optimal mechanisms by repeatedly sampling from the distribution. They obtain mechanisms that are approximately optimal and approximately incentive compatible.

One advantage of these computational approaches is that most of them are constructive so that one can systematically and computationally generate optimal mechanisms. However, a difficulty for most existing works in computer science (the second and third categories) is that mechanisms obtained in this way are either not optimal, or not truthful. A more desirable approach would be constructive on the one hand,

and able to return strictly incentive-compatible and (hopefully) strictly optimal mechanisms on the other hand.

2.1.2 Setting

We consider the problem of designing revenue-optimal auctions for the standard multi-item single-buyer setting. We follow the notations introduced in Chapter 1 and use v_i to denote the buyer's value for the i-th item (the index for the buyer is ignored for simplicity since there is only a single buyer). We adopt the standard additive, quasi-linear utility assumption (Equation (1.1)).

As mentioned in Section 1.1, any indirect mechanism has an equivalent truthful and direct mechanism. Furthermore, according to the *taxation principle*[20], any truthful mechanism can be represented as a *menu*. A menu is a set of tuples (or menu entries), each containing an allocation and a payment. After the menu is announced to the buyer, he chooses the menu entry that is the best for him.

Throughout this chapter, we use $[x, p]$ to denote a menu entry, where x is the allocation vector and p is the payment. If the buyer chooses the menu entry $[x, p]$, then his utility would be

$$u = \sum_i v_i x_i - p_i$$

Consider the following example:

Example 2.1 Suppose that the seller has two items for sale, and uses a menu containing the following items:

(1) $[(0, 0), 0]$;

(2) $[(1, 1), 1]$.

This mechanism belongs to the so-called bundling mechanisms, since it tries to sell the two items as a bundle.

To maximize his utility, the buyer chooses menu entry 1 if his value is $(0.4, 0.4)$, and chooses menu entry 2 if his value is $(0.8, 0.3)$, and is indifferent between the two menu entries if his value is $(0.3, 0.7)$.

Therefore, menus are just a special kind of indirect mechanisms, where the action set is exactly the menu entries. And according to the revelation principle and the taxation principle, it is without loss of generality to consider menus instead of directly designing both the allocation function and the payment function. We also define the following *naïve mechanisms*, which will be useful in defining our MENUNET structure.

Definition 2.1 (Naïve Mechanism) A naïve mechanism consists of an action set A and an associated mapping from any action to a possible outcome, i.e.,

$$(x, p) : A \mapsto \boldsymbol{X} \times \mathbb{R}_+$$

where $\boldsymbol{X}$ is the set of all possible allocations. In particular, there exists a special action $\perp$ meaning "exiting the mechanism" with

$$x(\perp) = 0, p(\perp) = 0$$

Note that in the multi-buyer case, the menu interpretation does not work anymore. Of course, we can change the representation so that the menu for each buyer depends on other buyers' values, but there can be conflicts when two buyers choose to buy the same item.

The "exit" menu entry $[0, 0] = [(0, \cdots, 0), 0]$ corresponds to the exiting action $\perp$. Note that the naïve mechanism with the menu presentation is a very general model of the mechanism design problem. In particular, even when the buyer is not fully rational, as long as the buyer follows a certain behavior model, the mechanism designer is still able to design the menu to maximize his objective. The robustness of naïve mechanisms is indeed critical to the flexibility and generality of this methodology.

For any naïve mechanism, the corresponding direct and truthful mechanism is

$$(\tilde{x}(v), \tilde{p}(v)) = s(v) = \arg\max_{a \in A} u(v, x(a), p(a))$$

where $s(v)$ is the buyer's strategy when his value is v. When there is no ambiguity, we use $\tilde{x}, \tilde{p}$ and x, p interchangeably for ease of presentation.

In this chapter, we focus on designing revenue optimal mechanisms for the seller, i.e., optimizing

$$\text{REV}(x, p) = \mathbb{E}_v [p(v)]$$

where the expectation is taken according to the buyer's value distribution F. Note that, different from the literature where F is commonly assumed to be independent among the items, we allow the value distribution F to be correlated. In fact, our networks allow for any type of value distributions.

Although we focus on the revenue of the mechanism, our method is not restricted to any specific objective function and can be applied to settings with other objective functions as well.

Revenue optimal mechanism design in multi-dimensional environments is a widely studied challenging problem. Hence applying our method in such a setting allows us to verify whether known results can be reproduced and whether unknown results can be found.

2.1.3 Revisiting the Naïve Mechanism

Although the revelation principle is widely adopted in the theoretical analysis of mechanism design problems to efficiently reduce the design space, we decide not to follow this approach when applying neural networks to solving such problems.

The main difficulty of directly following the approach based on traditional revelation principle is two-fold:

- It is unclear what network structure can directly encode the IC and IR constraints;
- Some of the characterization results for the additive valuation setting[①] can be cast into certain network structures, but such structures are restricted to additive valuation assumption and heavily rely on the domain knowledge of the specific mechanism design problem.

In fact, the above difficulties also limit the generality of the methods built on these elegant but specific characterizations. For example, there might be some fundamental challenges in generalizing such approaches to the settings where a buyer is risk-averse (or risk-seeking) or has partial (or bounded) rationality [21-24]. Furthermore, in many real world applications, the buyer behavior models may come from real data instead

---

① Such as Myerson's virtual value for single-dimensional settings and Rochet's increasing, convex and Lipschitz-1 buyer utility function for multi-dimensional settings [19].

of theoretical assumptions.

To circumvent these difficulties and guarantee a higher degree of flexibility, we build up our method from the most basic naïve mechanisms, by simply letting the buyer choose his favorite option.

To the best of our knowledge, our MENUNET is the first neural network-based approach that outputs a both IC and IR mechanism under multi-dimensional settings.

We now briefly explain how the naïve mechanism enables us to formulate a neural network-based approach for mechanism design. Intuitively, the naïve mechanism simply provides the buyer with various menu entries, i.e., allocations associated with different prices, and lets him choose the most preferred one. Once a buyer's utility function is specified (either by assumption or learned from data), his choice is simply an "argmax" of his utility function over possible action. As long as the utility function could be encoded by a neural network, which is a mild assumption, the buyer's behavior model can be represented by a neural network with an additional "argmax" layer①. For now, we can think of the encoded mechanism as a black-box network producing a set of (allocation, payment) pairs (see Figure 2.1). The pairs then are fed into a "buyer network". Finally, the "buyer network" outputs the choice which is used to evaluate the expected objective of the mechanism designer. The choices are weighted according to the probabilities of the corresponding value distribution and the training loss is simply the negated expected objective (given that the mechanism designer's goal is to maximize the objective).

Focusing on naïve mechanisms has the following advantages:

- We can obtain both the IC and IR properties for free. In a naïve mechanism, no additional constraints (such as IC and IR) are required. In fact, one difficulty of optimizing the direct mechanism network is that the violations of IC or IR constraints are not directly reflected in the designer's objective. Hence the standard optimization methods for neural networks do not

---

① Even if the buyer's utility function is not available, such a gadget could be replaced by any *behavior model* (given or learned from data) represented by a neural network instead of a utility function.

directly apply. In contrast, in the naïve mechanism network, any mechanism changes that affect the buyer's actions would be finally back-propagated to the mechanism network through the buyer network. The IC property is a natural consequence of the revelation principle and the taxation principle. The IR property is easily guaranteed due to the "exit" menu entry ⊥. Such properties facilitate the optimization in standard training methods of neural networks.

- The design space can be significantly reduced. Menus are a succinct representation of mechanisms and require much fewer parameters to describe the same mechanism compared to direct mechanisms.

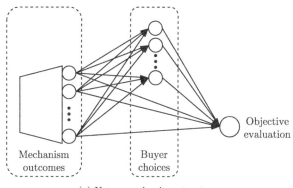

(a) Naïve mechanism structure

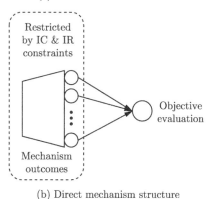

(b) Direct mechanism structure

Figure 2.1　A high-level abstraction of the neural networks

2.1.4 Network Structure of MENUNET

Our MENUNET contains two networks: the mechanism network and the buyer network. Since the networks represent a naïve mechanism, the output of the mechanism network is a set of menu entries, i.e., allocations along with different prices. The buyer network takes the set of menu entries as input and outputs his choice. The overall network structure is shown in Figure 2.2.

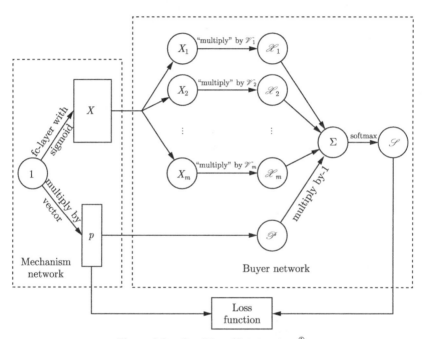

Figure 2.2   Our MenuNet structure[①]

2.1.4.1   Mechanism Network

Usually, a neural network takes a certain input x and then outputs a corresponding output y. However, our mechanism network is different from most neural networks in the sense that it outputs a set of menu entries, which already represents the entire mechanism. Therefore, our mechanism network does not actually need to take any input to give an

---

① The buyer network corresponds to a rational buyer with quasi-linear utility. In general cases, the buyer network can be constructed according to his utility function, or other networks trained from real data.

output. However, in order to fit in most neural network frameworks, we use a one-dimensional constant 1 as the input to our mechanism network. The output of the network consists of two parts. The first part is an allocation matrix X of m rows and k columns, where m is the number of items and k is the menu size (i.e., number of menu entries)[①]. Each column of X contains the allocation (can be either probabilistic or deterministic) of all m items. The second part is a payment vector p of length k, representing k prices for the k menu entries. The last column of the allocation matrix and the last element of the payment vector is always set to 0. This encodes the "exit" action of the buyer and ensures that the buyer can always have a non-negative utility by choosing this menu entry.

The structure of the mechanism network is simple enough. The constant input 1 goes through a fully connected layer to form each row X_i (except the last column, which is always 0) of the allocation matrix. We choose the sigmoid function as the activation function since the allocation of each item is always in $[0, 1]$. The payment vector is even simpler. Each element p_i of the payment vector is formed by multiplying the input constant with a scalar parameter. Therefore, the training of our network is very fast.

2.1.4.2 Buyer Network

The buyer network is a function that maps a mechanism to the buyer's strategy $s(v)$ (a distribution over all possible menu entries) for each value profile $v = (v_1, v_2, \cdots, v_m)$, where each v_i is the value of the i-th item. The output of the mechanism network (the allocation matrix X and the payment vector p) is taken as the input to the buyer network. To define the output of the buyer network, suppose that each v_i is bounded and $0 \leqslant v_i \leqslant \bar{v}_i$. We discretize the interval $[0, \bar{v}_i]$ to d_i discrete values. Let V_i be the set of possible discrete values of v_i and define $V = V_1 \times V_2 \times \cdots \times V_m$.

The output of the buyer network is a tensor of dimension $k \prod_{i=1}^{m} d_i$,

---

① The menu size k is a hyperparameter and cannot be trained. Of course, the mechanism network can possibly produce the optimal menu only when k is at least the size of the optimal menu. Note that in some cases (e.g., the buyer's values follow a beta distribution [16]), the size of the optimal menu is infinite, which cannot be handled by our network.

since the m-dimensional value profile has $\prod_{i=1}^{m} d_i$ distinct possible values and each possible value corresponds to k different outcomes. It is worth mentioning that the buyer's utility function is not necessary to build the buyer network, since the network only outputs the buyer's strategy, which may not even be consistent with any utility function.

The buyer network can be any network that has the same format of input and output as described above. When we do not know the buyer utility function but have plenty of interaction data (e.g., from the sponsored search), we can train a network to capture the buyer's behavior from the data.

When the buyer's utility function and behavioral model are known, we can manually design the buyer network structure so that the network outputs the buyer's strategy accurately. For example, in the case we consider, the buyer always chooses the menu entry that maximizes his utility function with probability 1. We then construct m tensors $\mathscr{V}_1, \cdots, \mathscr{V}_m$, each of dimension $\prod_{i=1}^{m} d_i$. The entry of index $j_1 j_2 \cdots j_m$ in $\mathscr{V}_i$ has value $v_i^{j_i}$, which is the j_i-th discretized value of the interval $[0, \bar{v}_i]$. Recall that X_i represents the allocations of the i-th item in the menu. By "multiplying" each $\mathscr{V}_i$ with X_i, we get a new tensor $\mathscr{X}_i$ of dimension $k \prod_{i=1}^{m} d_i$, where each element of the new tensor is the value of the i-th item obtained by choosing menu entry κ. By further adding the $\mathscr{X}_i$'s together, we get a tensor $\mathscr{X} = \sum_{i \in [m]} \mathscr{X}_i$, where the entry at index $j_1 j_2 \cdots j_m \kappa$ is the buyer's total value of choosing the κ-th menu entry while his value vector being $(v_1^{j_1}, \cdots, v_m^{j_m})$. Similarly, we also construct a payment tensor $\mathscr{P}$ of the same size, where each entry equals the payment of the κ-th menu entry.

Finally, we compute the utility tensor $\mathscr{U}$ by

$$\mathscr{U} = \left(\sum_{i \in [m]} \mathscr{X}_i \right) - \mathscr{P}$$

and then apply the softmax function across all the menu entries for each value profile in the utility tensor $\mathscr{U}$ to produce the output $\mathcal{S}$, an aggregation of $s(v), \forall v \in V$. For each value profile, the menu entry with the largest utility has the highest weight. We multiply the utility tensor by a large constant to make the weight of the best menu entry close enough to 1.

2.1.4.3   Loss Function

The loss function can be any function specified according to the mechanism designer's objective. In this chapter, we mainly focus on how to optimize the revenue of the mechanism and set the loss function to be the negated revenue.

Recall that the output of the buyer network is the buyer's strategy $s(v)$ for each value profile v. Then the loss function of the networks is

$$\mathrm{Loss} = -\mathrm{Rev}(x,p) = -\mathrm{E}_v \left[\boldsymbol{p}^{\mathrm{T}} s(v) \right]$$

Note that to compute the revenue, we need to aggregate all the discretized value profiles according to their corresponding probabilities. In other words, it is similar to enumerating all possible value profiles. Therefore discretization is necessary since we can not enumerate all values in a continuous space. This is similar to the previous linear programming approach[5,17].

As mentioned in Section 2.1.2, we do not make any assumption about the value distribution F. Our networks are able to handle both independent and correlated value distributions.

2.1.5   Recovering Known Results

In this section, we consider several settings with known optimal mechanisms. These settings are standard auction design settings with two items with a single buyer, and have closed-form optimal solutions. We apply our MENUNET to these settings and compare the solution given by the network with the optimal mechanism.

2.1.5.1   The Uniform Rectangle Setting

In this section, we consider the setting where the buyer's value (v_1, v_2) follows a uniform distribution over the rectangle $[0,c] \times [0,1]$ with $c \geqslant 1$. Note that for any case with $c < 1$, we can first consider the case with rectangle $[0, 1/c] \times [0, 1]$, and then normalize the value distribution and obtain the optimal mechanism by symmetry.

The optimal mechanism for this setting is known in closed-form[25]. We draw both the optimal mechanism and our experiment results together in Figure 2.3. The colored areas represent the mechanism given by our network, where each color corresponds to a different menu entry (the buyer chooses the menu entry if his value lies inside the corresponding colored area). The dashed line represents the optimal mechanism in theory (they are *not* drawn according to the colored areas).

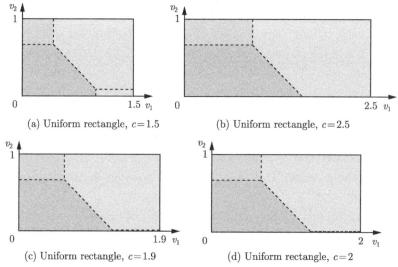

(a) Uniform rectangle, $c = 1.5$ (b) Uniform rectangle, $c = 2.5$

(c) Uniform rectangle, $c = 1.9$ (d) Uniform rectangle, $c = 2$

Figure 2.3   Computed solutions vs. optimal solutions for uniform distributions (see the color figure before)

How are these colored areas related to the allocation of each menu entry? Let $[(x_1, x_2), p]$ and $[(x_1', x_2'), p']$ be the corresponding menu entries of two adjacent colored areas. Consider two different points $v = (v_1, v_2)$ and $v' = (v_1', v_2')$ at the boundary of the two colored areas. A buyer with either v or v' is indifferent between the two menu entries:

$$v_1 x_1 + x_2 v_2 - p = v_1 x_1' + v_2 x_2' - p',$$

$$v_1' x_1 + x_2 v_2' - p = v_1' x_1' + v_2' x_2' - p'$$

Combining the above two equations we have

$$(v_1 - v_1')(x_1 - x_1') + (v_2 - v_2')(x_2 - x_2') = 0 \tag{2.1}$$

Therefore, the normal vector of the boundary line connecting v and v' is the changes in the allocation of the two menu entries.

In the uniform $[0, c] \times [0, 1]$ case, the origin point 0 always chooses the "exit" menu entry $[(0, 0), 0]$. According to Equation (2.1) and Figure 2.3, the optimal menu is always deterministic. Our experiment results are almost identical to the actual optimal mechanisms.

2.1.5.2   The Unit-Demand Buyer Setting

The unit-demand setting is also intensively studied in the literature. In this setting, the allocation must satisfy $x_1 + x_2 \leqslant 1$. Thirumulanathan et al.[26] provide detailed analysis and closed-form solutions in the unit-demand setting. With slight modifications, our mechanism network can also produce feasible and optimal allocations in this setting (Figure 2.4). Instead of applying the sigmoid function to each element of the allocation matrix, we apply a softmax function to each column (representing each menu entry) of the allocation matrix. However, with such a modification, the allocation satisfies $x_1 + x_2 = 1$ rather than $x_1 + x_2 \leqslant 1$. The solution is to add an extra dummy element to each column before applying the softmax function.

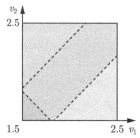

Figure 2.4   Solution comparison in the unit-demand setting
(see the color figure before)

2.1.5.3   The Grand Bundling Setting

One of the simplest mechanisms for selling multiple items is to sell them as a grand bundle. This case is equivalent to designing the optimal mechanism for selling a single item by viewing the grand bundle as a new "item". The buyer's value for the grand bundle can be obtained by computing the convolution of the value distribution functions of all the items. Therefore the optimal grand bundling mechanism is to set a posted price according to the value distribution of the grand bundle.

For simplicity, here we only consider the case with two items where the buyer's value distributions for the items are both $U[0,1]$. The experiment results are shown in Figure 2.5.

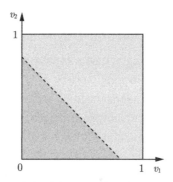

Figure 2.5   The grand bundling setting

2.2   Discovering Unknown Optimal Mechanisms

In the previous section, we designed MENUNET for solving optimal auction design problems, and applied them to some multi-item auction settings. Our network structure can handle not only the standard setting, but also settings with practical constraints (e.g., the unit-demand setting). The settings considered in Section 2.1 are those with known optimal mechanisms. As mentioned in Section 2.1, our aim was to demonstrate the ability of our network structure in discovering optimal mechanism, and to show that our framework was flexible enough to handle different settings.

In this section, we apply our MENUNET structure to some settings where the optimal auction mechanism is unknown. Given the effectiveness of our network structure shown in Section 2.1, our goal is to derive an analytic, closed-form optimal mechanism for some settings by analyzing the results provided by our neural networks.

2.2.1 Experiment Results

We now present the results of applying our MENUNET to the following settings: the correlated distribution setting where the buyer's value is distributed among a certain triangle (Section 2.2.1.1), the restricted menu size setting where the seller wants to decrease the complexity of the mechanism by reducing the menu size (Section 2.2.1.2), the combinatorial value setting where the buyer's value for the items is no longer additive (Section 2.2.1.3), and the deterministic menu setting where no lotteries are allowed in the mechanism (Section 2.2.1.4).

2.2.1.1 The Correlated Distribution Setting

Suppose that the buyer's value $v = (v_1, v_2)$ is uniformly distributed among the triangle described by $\left\{ (v_1, v_2) \mid \frac{v_1}{c} + v_2 \leqslant 1, v_1 \geqslant 0, v_2 \geqslant 0 \right\}$, where $c \geqslant 1$. Figure 2.6 shows the mechanisms given by our network. Note that in our framework, the joint value distribution is only used to compute the objective function. So our MENUNET can handle arbitrary value distributions. In fact, guided by these experiment results, we are able to find the closed-form optimal mechanism for this kind of value distributions[①]. In particular, there are two possible cases for this problem. When c is large, according to Equation (2.1), the optimal mechanism contains three menu entries and one of them is probabilistic. And when c is small, the optimal mechanism contains only two menu entries, i.e., use a posted price for the bundle of the items. Formally, we have:

Theorem 2.1 *When $c > \dfrac{4}{3}$, the optimal menu for the uniform triangle distribution contains the following items:* $[(0,0), 0]$, $\left[\left(\dfrac{1}{c}, 1 \right), \dfrac{2}{3} \right]$, *and* $\left[(1,1), \dfrac{2}{3}c - \dfrac{1}{3}\sqrt{c(c-1)} \right]$.

When $c \leqslant \dfrac{4}{3}$, the optimal menu for the uniform triangle distribution

---

① In a recent version, Dütting [27] followed our methodology to discover the optimal mechanisms for the uniform distribution on a shifted and scaled triangle $\{(v_1, v_2) \mid v_1/c + v_2 \leqslant 2, v_1 \geqslant 0, v_2 \geqslant 1\}$.

contains the following items: $[(0,0),0]$ *and* $\left[(1,1),\sqrt{\dfrac{c}{3}}\right].$

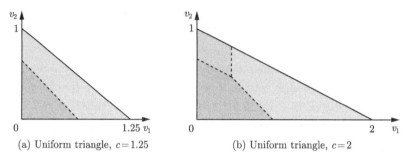

(a) Uniform triangle, $c=1.25$ (b) Uniform triangle, $c=2$

Figure 2.6   Computed solutions vs. optimal solutions for correlated distributions

Remark 2.1   Note that the condition $c > \dfrac{4}{3}$ guarantees that the price of the third menu entry is positive.

The proof of Theorem 2.1 is deferred to Section 2.2.2.

2.2.1.2   The Restricted Menu Size Setting

The output of our mechanism network is a set of menu entries. Thus we can control the menu size by directly setting the output size of the network.

Restricting the menu size results in simpler mechanisms. It is known that the size of the optimal menu could be infinitely large (containing uncountably many probabilistic menu entries) when the buyer's value for each item follows a beta distribution[16]. Such results directly motivate the study of simple mechanisms[3, 12], as they are easier to implement and optimize in practice.

We consider the case where the buyer's value is uniformly distributed in the unit square $[0,1] \times [0,1]$. It is known that the optimal mechanism contains 4 menu entries. Note that the grand bundling setting described in Section 2.1.5.3 is also a special case of this setting. However, the optimal mechanism for the case with at most 3 menu entries is unknown. The results given by our neural network are shown in Figure 2.7.

Surprisingly, when the menu can have at most 3 items, our network gives an asymmetric menu, despite that the value distribution is symmetric. In fact, we can also find the optimal menu with at most 3 items analytically. Our analysis shows that the optimal menu is indeed asymmetric. The intuition is that, if we add a symmetry constraint to the solution, then the optimal menu degenerates to a menu with only 2 items. We present the theoretical result here, but defer the proof to Section 2.2.2.

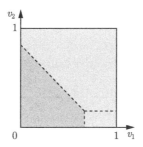

Figure 2.7   Uniform square with at most 3 menu entries

Theorem 2.2   *In a setting where the value profile of two additive items is uniformly distributed over the unit square* $[0, 1] \times [0, 1]$, *the optimal mechanism is to sell the first item at price* $\dfrac{2}{3}$ *or the bundle at price* $\dfrac{5}{6}$, *yielding revenue* $\dfrac{59}{108}$.

In addition, the optimal mechanism is unique except for its symmetric counterpart.

2.2.1.3   The Combinatorial Value Setting

Our MENUNET can also handle the case where the buyer has combinatorial utilities. Figure 2.8 shows the mechanism given by our network for a buyer with the following utility function:

$$u(v_1, v_2) = x_1 v_1 + x_2 v_2 + x_1 v_1 x_2 v_2 - p$$

In this case, the buyer's value for obtaining the items is not additive. We need to slightly modify the buyer network by adding the extra $x_1 v_1 x_2 v_2$ term, which can be easily implemented using standard neural network packages. Notice that in Figure 2.8, the dashed lines that are used to represent the actual optimal mechanisms are not drawn, as the optimal mechanism is still unknown.

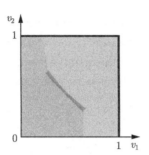

Figure 2.8   The combinatorial value setting
(see the color figure before)

2.2.1.4   The Deterministic Menu Setting

Similar to the case with restricted menu size, deterministic mechanisms are also important in practice, since they are easy to understand and implement. In this case, the mechanism network can be further simplified. For example, when selling 2 items, there can only be 4 possible deterministic menu entries, with the following 4 allocations $(0,0), (0,1), (1,0), (1,1)$. Therefore, the only parameters in the mechanism network are the corresponding prices.

Figure 2.9 shows our experiment results on uniform distributions over the triangle described in Section 2.2.1.1. By Theorem 2.1, the optimal mechanism is not deterministic when $c = 2$. With the deterministic constraint, our experiment shows that the revenue drops by 0.14%.

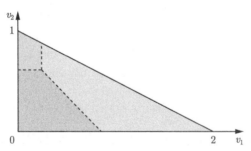

Figure 2.9   The deterministic menu setting

2.2.2   Theoretic Analysis and Formal Proofs

In this section, we provide theoretical proofs for some of our results. To the best of our knowledge, these results are previously unknown.

2.2.2.1　Proof of Theorem 2.1

As described in Section 2.2.1.1, there are two possible cases for the optimal mechanism when the buyer's value is uniformly distributed among the triangle.

We solve the problem case by case.

Theorem 2.3 (First part of Theorem 2.1) *For any* $c > \dfrac{4}{3}$, *suppose that the buyer's type is uniformly distributed among the set* $T = \{(v_1, v_2) \mid \dfrac{v_1}{c} + v_2 \leqslant 1, v_1 \geqslant 0, v_2 \geqslant 0\}$. *Then the optimal menu contains the following items:* $[(0,0), 0]$, $\left[\left(\dfrac{1}{c}, 1\right), \dfrac{2}{3}\right]$, *and* $\left[(1,1), \dfrac{2}{3}c - \dfrac{1}{3}\sqrt{c(c-1)}\right]$.

To prove Theorem 2.3, we apply the duality theory[16, 28] to our setting. We provide a brief description here and refer readers to Daskalakis et al.[16] and Daskalakis[28] for details. Let $f(v)$ be the joint value distribution, and V be the support of $f(v)$. Define measures μ_0, μ_∂, μ_s as follows:

- μ_0 has a point mass at $v = 0$;
- μ_∂ is only distributed along the boundary of V, with density $f(v)(v \cdot \eta(v))$, where $\eta(v)$ is the outer unit normal vector at v;
- μ_s is distributed in V with a density $\nabla f(v) \cdot v + (m+1)f(v)$, where m is the number of items.

Let $\mu = \mu_0 + \mu_\partial - \mu_s$, μ_+ and μ_- be two non-negative measures such that $\mu = \mu_+ - \mu_-$, and V_+ and V_- be the support sets of μ_+ and μ_-. Daskalakis[28] shows that an optimal mechanism for selling m items to 1 buyer can be found by solving the following program:

$$\sup \quad \int_V u \, \mathrm{d}\mu_+ - \int_V u \, \mathrm{d}\mu_-$$

$$\text{s.t.} \quad u(v) - u(v') \leqslant \|(v - v')_+\|_1, \forall v \in V_+, v' \in V_- \qquad \text{(P)}$$

$$u \text{ is convex,} \quad u(\underline{v}) = 0$$

where $u(v)$ is the utility of the buyer when his value is v, $\|(v - v')_+\|_1 = \sum_{i=1}^{n} \max(0, v_i - v'_i)$, and $\underline{v}$ is the smallest possible value profile.

Relax the above program by removing the convexity constraint and write the dual program of the relaxed program:

$$\inf \quad \int_{V \times V} \|(v - v')_+\|_1 \, d\gamma \tag{D}$$

$$\text{s.t.} \quad \gamma \in \Gamma(\mu_+, \mu_-)$$

where $\Gamma(\mu_+, \mu_-)$ is the set of non-negative measures γ defined over $V \times V$ such that, for any $V' \subseteq V$, the following equations hold:

$$\int_{V' \times V} d\gamma = \mu_+(V'), \quad \int_{V \times V'} d\gamma = \mu_-(V')$$

Lemma 2.1 (Daskalakis et al. [16]) (D) *is a weak dual of* (P).

We omit the proof here but refer readers to Daskalakis et al. [16] and Daskalakis [28] for details. The dual program (D) has an optimal transport interpretation. We "move" the mass from μ_+ to other points to form μ_- and the measure γ corresponds to the amount of mass that goes from each point to another in V.

Although (D) is only a weak dual of (P), we can still use it to certify the optimality of a solution. We already give a menu in Theorem 2.1. Therefore, the relaxed convexity constraint is automatically satisfied if the buyer always chooses the best menu entry.

In our case of $f(v) = \dfrac{2}{c}$, we have: $V = T, \underline{v} = (0, 0)$, μ_∂ has a constant line density of $\dfrac{2}{\sqrt{1 + c^2}}$ along the segment $\dfrac{v_1}{c} + v_2 = 1, 0 \leqslant v_2 \leqslant 1$, and μ_s has a constant density of $\dfrac{6}{c}$ over T.

Let R_i be the region of T such that for any $v \in R_i$, choosing menu entry i maximizes the buyer's utility.

It is straightforward to verify that the measures μ_+ and μ_- are balanced inside each region, i.e., $\mu_+(R_i) = \mu_-(R_i), \forall i$. Therefore, the transport of mass only happens inside each region.

We construct the transport in R_1 and R_2 as follows:

- R_1: μ_+ is concentrated on a single point 0, We move the mass at 0 uniformly to all points in R_1.

- R_2: μ_+ is only distributed along the upper boundary of R_2. For each point v at the upper boundary, we draw a vertical line l through it, and move the mass at v uniformly to the points in $L \cap R_2$.

However, for R_3, μ_+ is also only distributed along the upper boundary, but there is no easy transport as for R_1 and R_2. We provide the following Lemma 2.2.

Lemma 2.2 *For R_3, there exists a transport of mass, such that for any two points v, v', if there is non-negative transport from v to v', then $v_i \geqslant v'_i, \forall i$.*

Proof Denote the upper boundary of R_3 by B. For each $v \in B$, define

$$R_L = \{v' \in R_3 \mid v'_1 \leqslant v_1\}, \quad R_U = \{v' \in R_3 \mid v'_2 \geqslant v_2\}$$

For any line l_v through v with a non-negative slope (or infinity), denote the part of R_3 that is above the line by R_v. It is easy to verify that $\mu_+(R_U) \geqslant \mu_-(R_U)$ and $\mu_+(R_L) \leqslant \mu_-(R_L)$. Thus there exists a line l_v^* such that the corresponding R_v^* satisfies $\mu_+(R_v^*) = \mu_-(R_v^*)$.

Now we show that for any two v and v', the intersection point of l_v^* and $l_{v'}^*$ is not inside R_3. In Figure 2.10, the three regions R_1, R_2, R_3 are the quadrangles $OIDE$, $YCDI$, and $CDEX$, respectively. Let points A, B correspond to the value profiles v and v'. Assume, on the contrary, that the intersection point of l_v^* (line AA') and $l_{v'}^*$ (line BB') is inside R_3. Then we have

$$\mu_+(ACDA') = \mu_-(ACDA'), \quad \mu_+(BCDB') = \mu_-(BCDB') \qquad (2.2)$$

Note that μ_+ is only distributed along the line CX inside R_3. Thus

$$\mu_+(BCDA') = \mu_+(BCDB') = \mu_-(BCDB') \qquad (2.3)$$

However, μ_- has a positive density inside R_3. Therefore, we have

$$\mu_-(BCDA') > \mu_-(BCDB') \qquad (2.4)$$

Combining Equation (2.2), (2.3) and (2.4), we obtain

$$\mu_+(BAA') < \mu_-(BAA') \qquad (2.5)$$

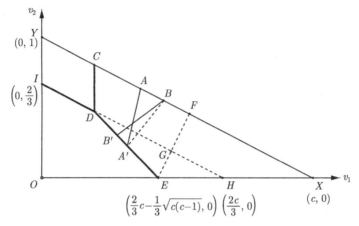

Figure 2.10 The intersection point of l_v^* and $l_{v'}^*$

Since μ_+ is uniformly distributed along the line CX with density $\dfrac{2}{\sqrt{1+c^2}}$, we have that $\mu_+(BAA') = \dfrac{2}{\sqrt{1+c^2}} \cdot l(AB)$, where $l(\cdot)$ denotes the length of a segment. Similarly, $\mu_-(BAA') = \dfrac{6}{c} \cdot S(BAA')$, where $S(BAA')$ is the area of triangle BAA'. Let h be the altitude of the triangle BAA' with respect to the base AB. So

$$S(BAA') = \frac{1}{2}l(AB) \cdot h \leqslant \frac{1}{2}l(AB) \cdot l(EF) = l(AB) \cdot \frac{c + \sqrt{c(c-1)}}{6\sqrt{1+c^2}}$$

where line EF is perpendicular to line CX. Then

$$\mu_-(BAA') = \frac{6}{c} \cdot S(BAA')$$

$$\leqslant \frac{6}{c} \cdot l(AB) \cdot \frac{c + \sqrt{c(c-1)}}{6\sqrt{1+c^2}}$$

$$= l(AB) \cdot \frac{c + \sqrt{c(c-1)}}{c\sqrt{1+c^2}}$$

$$\leqslant l(AB) \cdot \frac{2}{\sqrt{1+c^2}}$$

$$= \mu_+(BAA'),$$

which contradicts to Equation (2.5).

Consider the set of lines $K = \{l_v^* \mid v \in B\}$. Since we have already shown that no two of these lines have an intersection point inside R_3, the line set K actually cuts the region R_3 into "slices". And for any "slice" s, we have $\mu_+(s) = \mu_-(s)$. Therefore, for each point in B, we can find its corresponding "slice" and move its mass uniformly to all the points inside the "slice". And since l_v^* always has a non-negative (or infinite) slope, we conclude that whenever there is a mass transport from v to v', we have $v_i \geqslant v_i', \forall i$.

With this lemma, we can simplify our proof of Theorem 2.1, and do not need to construct the measure γ explicitly.

Proof (Proof of Theorem 2.3)   We first compute the revenue of the mechanism given by Theorem 2.3, i.e., the objective of the primal program. Point D in Figure 2.10 has coordinates (x_D, y_D), where $x_D = \frac{2}{3}c - \frac{1}{3}\sqrt{c(c-1)} - \frac{1}{3}\sqrt{\frac{c}{c-1}}$ and $y_D = \frac{1}{3}\sqrt{\frac{c}{c-1}}$.

Therefore, we have

$$\Pr\{\text{The buyer chooses menu item 2}\} = f(v) \cdot S(YCDI) = \frac{2}{c} \cdot \frac{1}{3}x_D$$

$$\Pr\{\text{The buyer chooses menu item 3}\} = f(v) \cdot S(CDEX)$$

$$= \frac{2}{c}\left[\frac{c}{2}\left(\frac{1}{3} + y_D\right)^2 - \frac{1}{2}y_D^2\right]$$

Thus the revenue of the menu provided in Theorem 2.3 is

$$\text{REV} = \frac{2}{3} \cdot \Pr\{\text{The buyer chooses menu item 2}\}+$$

$$\left(\frac{2}{3}c - \frac{1}{3}\sqrt{c(c-1)}\right) \cdot \Pr\{\text{The buyer chooses menu item 3}\}$$

$$= \frac{2}{27}\left[4 + c + \sqrt{c(c-1)}\right]$$

Now we compute the objective of the dual program (D). And to prove the optimality of the menu, it suffices to show that the objective of (D) is equal to REV.

Note that in our construction of the transport in R_1 and R_2, we only allow transport inside each region. In R_1, we transport mass from point

0 to other points. So it does not contribute to the objective of (D), and we can just ignore R_1. In R_2, the mass is always moved vertically down. Therefore, for any v, v', such that there is positive mass transport from v to v', we have $v_i \geqslant v'_i, \forall i$ and $\|(v - v')_+\|_1 = \sum_i \max(0, v_i - v'_i) = \sum_i (v_i - v'_i) = \sum_i (v_i - 0) - \sum_i (v'_i - 0)$. Therefore,

$$\int_{R_2 \times R_2} \|(v - v')_+\|_1 \, \mathrm{d}\gamma = \int_{R_2 \times R_2} \|v - 0\|_1 \, \mathrm{d}\gamma - \int_{R_2 \times R_2} \|v' - 0\|_1 \, \mathrm{d}\gamma \tag{2.6}$$

For the first term, we have

$$\int_{R_2 \times R_2} \|v - 0\|_1 \, \mathrm{d}\gamma = \int_{R_2 \times T} \|v - 0\|_1 \, \mathrm{d}\gamma = \sum_j \int_{\sigma_j \times T} \|v - 0\|_1 \, \mathrm{d}\gamma$$

where the first equation is due to the fact that our transport is inside each region, and $\{\sigma_j\}$ is a partition of the region R_2. When the maximum area of σ_j approaches 0, we get

$$\int_{R_2 \times R_2} \|v - 0\|_1 \, \mathrm{d}\gamma = \int_{R_2} \|v - 0\|_1 \, \mathrm{d}\mu_+$$
$$= \int_0^{x_D} \left(v_1 + 1 - \frac{v_1}{c} \right) \frac{2}{\sqrt{1 + c^2}} \frac{\sqrt{1 + c^2}}{c} \, \mathrm{d}v_1$$
$$= \frac{1}{9} \left[8 - 6\sqrt{\frac{c}{c - 1}} + 5c - 4\sqrt{c(c - 1)} \right]$$

Similarly, the second term of Equation (2.6) is

$$\int_{R_2 \times R_2} \|v' - 0\|_1 \, \mathrm{d}\gamma = \int_{R_2} \|v' - 0\|_1 \, \mathrm{d}\mu_-$$
$$= \frac{(2\sqrt{c - 1} - \sqrt{c}) \left[3 + 2c - \sqrt{c(c - 1)} \right]}{9\sqrt{c - 1}}$$

For R_3, according to Lemma 2.2, it is also true that when there is positive mass transport from v to v', we always have $v_i \geqslant v'_i, \forall i$. Therefore,

$$\int_{R_3 \times R_3} \|(v - v')_+\|_1 \, \mathrm{d}\gamma = \int_{R_3 \times R_3} \|v - 0\|_1 \, \mathrm{d}\gamma - \int_{R_3 \times R_3} \|v' - 0\|_1 \, \mathrm{d}\gamma$$

For the first term,

$$\int_{R_3 \times R_3} \|v - 0\|_1 \, d\gamma = \int_{x_D}^{c} \left(v_1 + 1 - \frac{v_1}{c} \right) \frac{2}{c} \, dv_1$$

$$= \frac{1}{9} \left(1 + 4c + \frac{4c\sqrt{c}}{c-1} + 2\sqrt{\frac{c}{c-1}} \right)$$

Similarly, for the second term,

$$\int_{R_3 \times R_3} \|v' - 0\|_1 \, d\gamma = \int_{v \in R_3} \frac{6}{c}(v_1 + v_2) \, dv$$

$$= \frac{1}{27} \left(1 + 5\sqrt{\frac{c}{c-1}} + 10c + 10c\sqrt{\frac{c}{c-1}} \right)$$

Therefore, the objective of the dual program (D) is

$$\int_{T \times T} \|(v - v')_+\|_1 d\gamma = \int_{R_2 \times R_2} \|(v - v')_+\|_1 d\gamma + \int_{R_3 \times R_3} \|(v - v')_+\|_1 d\gamma$$

$$= \frac{2}{27} \left[4 + c + \sqrt{c(c-1)} \right]$$

$$= \text{Rev}$$

The above equation shows that the dual objective is equal to the actual revenue, which certifies that the menu is optimal.

When $c \leqslant \frac{4}{3}$, the optimal mechanism only has two menu entries.

Theorem 2.4 (Second part of Theorem 2.1) *For any $1 \leqslant c \leqslant \frac{4}{3}$, suppose that the buyer's type is uniformly distributed among the set $T = \left\{ (v_1, v_2) \mid \frac{v_1}{c} + v_2 \leqslant 1, v_1 \geqslant 0, v_2 \geqslant 0 \right\}$. Then the optimal menu contains the following two items: $[(0,0), 0]$ and $\left[(1,1), \sqrt{\frac{c}{3}} \right]$.*

One can prove Theorem 2.4 with the same trick as in Lemma 2.2. We omit the proof of this theorem since it is easier compared to Theorem 2.3.

2.2.2.2 Proof of Theorem 2.2

We now consider the optimal menu with at most three entries for value distribution $U[0,1]^2$. We omit the proof of the case where the menu has at most 2 entries.

Theorem 2.5 *The optimal symmetric mechanism of menu size at most three for two additive items with $v \sim U[0,1]^2$ is to sell the bundle of two items at the price of* $\dfrac{\sqrt{6}}{3}$, *yielding revenue of* $\dfrac{2\sqrt{6}}{9} \approx 0.54433$.

Proof   Since $[(0,0),0]$ must be one of the three symmetric menus, the other two must have the form of $[(\alpha,\beta),p]$ and $[(\beta,\alpha),p]$.

Without loss of generality, we assume that $\alpha \geqslant \beta$ and $\alpha > 0$ (otherwise $\alpha = \beta = 0$, yielding 0 revenue). Therefore, if $\alpha v_1 + \beta v_2 < p$ and $\beta v_1 + \alpha v_2 < p$, the buyer will choose the zero menu $[(0,0),0]$. We prove the result case by case.

Case 1 $p \leqslant \alpha$. In this case, we have

$$\Pr\{\alpha v_1 + \beta v_2 < p \text{ and } \beta v_1 + \alpha v_2 < p\}$$

$$= 2 \cdot \Pr\{\alpha v_1 + \beta v_2 < p \text{ and } v_1 \geqslant v_2\}$$

$$= \frac{p}{\alpha} \cdot \frac{p}{\alpha + \beta}$$

The corresponding revenue is

$$\text{REV} = p \cdot \Pr\{\text{the buyer does not choose the zero menu}\}$$

$$= \left(1 - \frac{p^2}{\alpha(\alpha + \beta)}\right) \cdot p$$

$$= \left(1 - \frac{p^2}{\alpha^2} \cdot \frac{1}{1 + \beta/\alpha}\right) \cdot p$$

$$\leqslant \left(1 - \frac{p^2}{2}\right) \cdot p$$

$$= \sqrt{\left(1 - \frac{p^2}{2}\right) \cdot \left(1 - \frac{p^2}{2}\right) \cdot p^2}$$

$$\leqslant \frac{2\sqrt{6}}{9}$$

The first inequality becomes an equality if and only if $\alpha = \beta = 1$ and the second one becomes an equality if and only if $1 - \dfrac{p^2}{2} = p^2$, which is equivalent to $p = \sqrt{\dfrac{2}{3}}$.

Case 2 $p \geqslant \alpha$. In this case, we have

$$\Pr\{\alpha v_1 + \beta v_2 < p \text{ and } \beta v_1 + \alpha v_2 < p\}$$

$$= 2\Pr\{\alpha v_1 + \beta v_2 < p \text{ and } v_1 \geqslant v_2\}$$

$$= \frac{p}{\alpha} \cdot \frac{p}{\alpha + \beta} + \left(\frac{p}{\alpha} - 1\right)^2$$

Hence

$$\mathrm{REV} = \left[1 - \frac{p^2}{\alpha^2} \cdot \frac{1}{1 + \beta/\alpha} + \left(\frac{p}{\alpha} - 1\right)^2\right] \cdot p$$

$$\leqslant \left[1 - \frac{p^2}{\alpha^2} \cdot \frac{1}{2} + \left(\frac{p}{\alpha} - 1\right)^2\right] \cdot p$$

$$= \frac{p}{2}\left(\frac{p^2}{\alpha^2} - 4 \cdot \frac{p}{\alpha} + 4\right)$$

Let $x = \dfrac{p}{\alpha} \geqslant 1$, the right-hand-side becomes

$$\frac{\alpha}{2}(x^3 - 4x^2 + 4x) \leqslant \frac{1}{2}(x^3 - 4x^2 + 4x)$$

Then consider the first order derivative of $x^3 - 4x^2 + 4x$:

$$(x^3 - 4x^2 + 4x)' = 3x^2 - 8x + 4 = (3x - 2)(x - 2)$$

the local maximum is reached at $x = \dfrac{2}{3}$. Note that in this case, $x = \dfrac{p}{\alpha} \geqslant$ 1. Hence the maximum revenue conditional on $p \geqslant \alpha$ is reached when $p = \alpha = \beta = 1$, where $\mathrm{REV} = \dfrac{1}{2} < \dfrac{2\sqrt{6}}{9}$.

Theorem 2.5 shows that the optimal symmetric 3-entry menu ends up being the degenerate case with 2 entries.

Now we move to the asymmetric case (Theorem 2.2). First, let's restate the theorem as follows.

Theorem 2.6 (Theorem 2.2 restated) *The optimal at-most-three-menu mechanism for two additive items with distribution $U[0,1]^2$*

is to sell the first item at price $\dfrac{2}{3}$ *or the bundle of the two items at price* $\dfrac{5}{6}$, *yielding revenue* $\dfrac{59}{108} \approx 0.546296$.

By symmetry, the mechanism could also be selling the second item at price $\dfrac{2}{3}$ *or the bundle of the two items at price* $\dfrac{5}{6}$. *In particular, there is no other at-most-three-menu mechanism that could generate as much revenue as they do.*

We prove Theorem 2.2 through the basic parametric method. Note that there must be a zero menu entry $Z = [(0,0),0]$, and hence we have two menu entries to determine. Suppose that the remaining two menu entries are $A = [(\alpha,\beta),p]$ and $B = [(\gamma,\delta),q]$. We then solve the following problem:

$$\begin{aligned} \max \quad & \text{Rev}(A,B,Z) \\ \text{s.t.} \quad & \alpha,\beta,\gamma,\delta \in [0,1], \ p,q \geqslant 0 \end{aligned} \qquad \text{(3Menu)}$$

To establish the connection between the menu and the revenue, let S_A be the set of values that menu entry A is preferred:

$$S_A = \{(v_1,v_2) \,|\, (v_1,v_2) \cdot (\alpha,\beta) - p \geqslant (v_1,v_2) \cdot (\gamma,\delta) - q$$
$$\text{and } (v_1,v_2) \cdot (\alpha,\beta) - p \geqslant 0\}$$

Similarly, we define S_B and S_Z to be the set of values where menu entry B and menu entry Z are preferred, respectively:

$$S_B = \{(v_1,v_2) \,|\, (v_1,v_2) \cdot (\gamma,\delta) - q \geqslant (v_1,v_2) \cdot (\alpha,\beta) - p$$
$$\text{and } (v_1,v_2) \cdot (\gamma,\delta) - q \geqslant 0\}$$
$$S_Z = \{(v_1,v_2) \,|\, (v_1,v_2) \cdot (\alpha,\beta) - p \leqslant 0$$
$$\text{and } (v_1,v_2) \cdot (\gamma,\delta) - q \leqslant 0\}$$

For any set $S \subseteq [0,1]^2$, let $|S| = \Pr\{(v_1,v_2) \in S\}$ be its probabilistic measure. Then the revenue of the mechanism with menu items A, B, and Z is

$$\text{Rev}(A,B,Z) = |S_A| \cdot p + |S_B| \cdot q \qquad (2.7)$$

There are two major challenges in solving the program (3Menu):

- There are too many cases with different formulas of $|S_A|$ and $|S_B|$, hence the formula of $\text{REV}(A, B, Z)$. In particular, there are 4 possible intersection patterns between the boundary of the square $[0, 1]^2$ and the intersections of every two menu entries ($S_A \cap S_B$, $S_B \cap S_Z$, $S_Z \cap S_Z$). So there are roughly $4^3 = 64$ different cases in total.
- Even within each specific case, the revenue REV is still a high-order function with 6 variables. In general, there is no guarantee that closed-form solutions exist.

To overcome the two challenges, the following lemmas are critical in reducing both the number of different cases and free variables.

Lemma 2.3   *Without loss of generality, the optimal mechanism of menu size at most three includes bundling $(1, 1)$ as one menu entry.*

Proof   Without loss of generality, suppose $p \geqslant q$, and then there must be an optimal mechanism with $\alpha = \beta = 1$. Because by replacing menu A with menu $A' = [(1, 1), p]$, the set of values where A' dominating B and Z, $S'_{A'}$ will be a superset of S_A, and similarly, S'_Z will be a subset of S_Z, i.e., $S'_{A'} \supseteq S_A$ and $S'_Z \subseteq S_Z$. Therefore,

$$
\begin{aligned}
\text{REV}' &= |S'_{A'}| \cdot p + |S'_B| \cdot q \\
&= |S'_{A'}| \cdot (p - q) + (1 - |S'_Z|) \cdot q \\
&\geqslant |S_A| \cdot (p - q) + (1 - |S_Z|) \cdot q \\
&= \text{REV}
\end{aligned}
$$

Lemma 2.4 (Pavlov[29])   *For $v \sim U[0, 1]^2$, consider a mechanism with a menu entry $[(\gamma, \delta), q]$ such that $\gamma, \delta \neq 1$ and $(\gamma, \delta) \neq (0, 0)$, then by replacing the menu entry with $[(\gamma', \delta'), q']$ (the price q' may also be different), the revenue of the new mechanism is no less than the original, where $\gamma' = 1$ or $\delta' = 1$ or $(\gamma', \delta') = (0, 0)$.*

Before we prove Theorem 2.2, let's consider 3 special cases as follows (see Figure 2.11).

Lemma 2.5 (Case 1)   *Conditioned on $p \leqslant 1$, the optimal mechanism consists of three asymmetric menu entries:*

$$
A : [(1, 1), 5/6], \quad B : [(1, 0), 2/3], \quad Z : [(0, 0), 0]
$$

which yield revenue $\dfrac{59}{108}$.

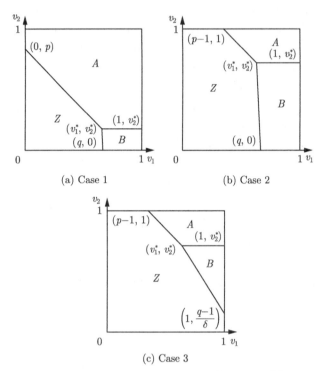

(a) Case 1   (b) Case 2

(c) Case 3

Figure 2.11   Three possible cases of Theorem 2.2

Proof   When $p \leqslant 1$, consider the intersection points:

$$S_B \cap S_Z \cap \{v \mid v_2 = 0\} = \{(q, 0)\} \quad \text{and}$$

$$S_A \cap S_B \cap \{v \mid v_1 = 1\} = \left\{ \left(1, \frac{p - q}{1 - \delta} \right) \right\}$$

Note that $q \leqslant p \leqslant 1$, we have

$$|S_B| = \frac{1}{2} \left[(1 - q) \cdot v_2^* + \frac{p - q}{1 - \delta} \cdot (1 - v_1^*) \right],$$

$$|S_Z| = \frac{1}{2} \left[p^2 - (p - q) \cdot v_2^* \right],$$

$$|S_A| = 1 - |S_B| - |S_Z|$$

Then the revenue is

$$\text{REV} = (1 - |S_Z|) \cdot p - |S_B| \cdot (p - q)$$

$$= \frac{1}{2} \left[2p - p^3 + (p-q)p \cdot v_2^* - (1-q)(p-q) \cdot v_2^* - \frac{(p-q)^2}{1-\delta}(1-v_1^*) \right]$$

$$= \frac{1}{2} \left[2p - p^3 - \frac{(p-q)^3}{(1-\delta)^2} + \frac{(p-q)^2(2p+q-2)}{1-\delta} \right]$$

$$= \frac{1}{2} \left(2p - p^3 + (p-q)^3 \cdot \left\{ - \left[\frac{1}{1-\delta} - \frac{2p+q-2}{2(p-q)} \right]^2 + \right. \right.$$

$$\left. \left. \left[\frac{2p+q-2}{2(p-q)} \right]^2 \right\} \right)$$

$$\leqslant \frac{1}{2} \left[2p - p^3 + (p-q)\left(p + \frac{q}{2} - 1\right)^2 \right]$$

where the upper bound is reached if and only if $p = q$ and $1 - \delta = \dfrac{2(p-q)}{(2p+q-2)}$.

Remember that we have shown that $p \neq q$, hence we must have

$$1 - \delta = \frac{2(p-q)}{(2p+q-2)}$$

and

$$2\text{REV} = 2p - p^3 + (p-q)\left(p + \frac{q}{2} - 1\right)^2$$

$$= 2p - p^3 + (p-q)\left(p + \frac{q}{2} - 1\right)\left(p + \frac{q}{2} - 1\right)$$

$$\leqslant 2p - p^3 + \left[\frac{1}{3}(p-q) + \left(p + \frac{q}{2} - 1\right) + \left(p + \frac{q}{2} - 1\right) \right]^3$$

$$= 2p - p^3 + \left(p - \frac{2}{3}\right)^3$$

where the upper bound is reached if and only if $p - q = p + \dfrac{q}{2} - 1$, or equivalently $q = \dfrac{2}{3}$. Therefore,

$$\text{REV} = -p^2 + \frac{5}{3}p - \frac{4}{27} \leqslant -\left(p - \frac{5}{6}\right)^2 + \frac{25}{36} - \frac{4}{27}$$

And its local maximum is reached when $p = \dfrac{5}{6}$, hence the optimal revenue is

$$\text{REV} = \frac{59}{108} \approx 0.546296 > \frac{2\sqrt{6}}{9} \approx 0.54433$$

and the menu entries are

$$A : [(1,1), 5/6] \quad B : [(1,0), 2/3] \quad Z : [(0,0), 0]$$

Lemma 2.6 (Case 2) *Conditioned on $p \geqslant 1 > q$, the optimal mechanism yields revenue* $\dfrac{14}{27}$.

　　　Proof When $p > 1 \geqslant q$, consider the intersection points:

$$S_B \cap S_Z \cap \{v \mid v_2 = 0\} = \{v = (q, 0)\},$$

$$S_A \cap S_B \cap \{v \mid v_1 = 1\} = \left\{v = \left(1, \frac{p-q}{1-\delta}\right)\right\}$$

Hence

$$|S_B| = \frac{1}{2}\left[(1-q) \cdot v_2^* + \frac{p-q}{1-\delta} \cdot (1 - v_1^*)\right],$$

$$|S_Z| = 1 - |S_A| - |S_B|,$$

$$|S_A| = \frac{1}{2}\left\{(2-p)^2 - \left[\frac{p-q}{1-\delta} - (p-1)\right](1 - v_1^*)\right\}$$

Thus the revenue is

$$\begin{aligned}
\text{REV} &= |S_A| \cdot p + |S_B| \cdot q \\
&= \frac{1}{2}\left\{3p - 2p^2 + (p-q)^2 \cdot \left[-\frac{p-q}{(1-\delta)^2} + \frac{2p+q-2}{1-\delta}\right]\right\}
\end{aligned}$$

$$= \frac{1}{2} \left(3p - 2p^2 + (p-q)^3 \cdot \left\{ -\left[\frac{1}{1-\delta} - \frac{2p+q-2}{2(p-q)} \right]^2 + \right. \right.$$

$$\left. \left. \left[\frac{2p+q-2}{2(p-q)} \right]^2 \right\} \right)$$

$$\leqslant \frac{1}{2} \left[3p - 2p^2 + (p-q) \left(p + \frac{q}{2} - 1 \right)^2 \right]$$

$$\leqslant \frac{3}{2}p - p^2 + \frac{1}{2} \left(p - \frac{2}{3} \right)^3 \tag{2.8}$$

$$= \frac{1}{54} \left(27p^3 - 108p^2 + 117p - 8 \right) \tag{2.9}$$

where the two inequalities become equalities if and only if

$$1 - \delta = \frac{2(p-q)}{2p+q-2}, \quad q = \frac{2}{3}$$

Note that we have to ensure $v_2^* \leqslant 1$, which is equivalent to $\frac{p-q}{1-\delta} \leqslant 1$, in other words,

$$\frac{\left(p - \frac{2}{3} \right) \left(p + \frac{1}{3} - 1 \right)}{p - \frac{2}{3}} \leqslant 1$$

thus $p \leqslant \frac{5}{3}$.

Now consider the maximum of the right-hand side of Equation (2.9) $\frac{1}{54}(27p^3 - 108p^2 + 117p - 8)$ in the interval $\left[1, \frac{5}{3} \right]$. By the first order condition, the local maximum and minimum are reached at $p = \frac{4-\sqrt{3}}{3} \approx$ 0.75598 < 1 and $p = \frac{4+\sqrt{3}}{3} \approx 1.91068 > \frac{5}{3}$, respectively. Therefore, in this case, the revenue is decreasing in p and hence the maximum revenue is reached at $p = 1$, and the maximum revenue is $\text{REV} = \frac{14}{27} < \frac{59}{108}$.

Lemma 2.7 (Case 3) *Conditioned on $p > q > 1$, the optimal revenue is no more than $\dfrac{1}{2}$.*

Proof   When $p > q > 1$, consider the intersection points:

$$S_B \cap S_Z \cap \{v \mid v_1 = 1\} = \left\{ v_1 = 1, v_2 = \frac{q-1}{\delta} \right\},$$

$$S_A \cap S_B \cap \{v \mid v_1 = 1\} = \left\{ v_1 = 1, v_2 = \frac{p-q}{1-\delta} \right\}$$

Hence

$$\begin{cases} |S_B| = \dfrac{1}{2}\left(\dfrac{p-q}{1-\delta} - \dfrac{q-1}{\delta} \right)(1 - v_1^*) \\[2mm] |S_Z| = 1 - |S_A| - |S_B| \\[2mm] |S_A| = \dfrac{1}{2}\left\{ (2-p)^2 - \left[\dfrac{p-q}{1-\delta} - (p-1) \right](1 - v_1^*) \right\} \end{cases}$$

Note that in this case, both S_A and S_B are non-empty, thus we have $v_2^* < 1$ and $v_1^* < 1$, hence:

$$\frac{p-q}{1-\delta} < 1 \tag{2.10}$$

$$\frac{q-\delta p}{1-\delta} < 1 \tag{2.11}$$

Therefore,

$$\frac{p-q}{1-\delta} = p - \frac{q-\delta p}{1-\delta} > p - 1$$

Then the revenue is

$$\begin{aligned} \text{Rev} &= |S_A| \cdot p + |S_B| \cdot q \\ &= \frac{1}{2}\left((2-p)^2 \cdot p + \left\{ -\left[\frac{p-q}{1-\delta} - (p-1) \right]p + \right.\right.\\ &\quad \left.\left. \left(\frac{p-q}{1-\delta} - \frac{q-1}{\delta} \right)q \right\}(1 - v_1^*) \right) \end{aligned}$$

$$\leqslant \frac{1}{2}\left((2-p)^2 \cdot p + \left\{-\left[\frac{p-q}{1-\delta} - (p-1)\right]q + \right.\right.$$

$$\left.\left.\left(\frac{p-q}{1-\delta} - \frac{q-1}{\delta}\right)q\right\}(1-v_1^*)\right)$$

$$= \frac{1}{2}\left[(2-p)^2 \cdot p + \left(p-1-\frac{q-1}{\delta}\right)\left(1-\frac{q-\delta p}{1-\delta}\right)q\right]$$

Meanwhile, note that by Equation (2.10), $v_2^* = \frac{p-q}{1-\delta} < 1$, hence $1 - v_1^* = 1 - (p - v_2^*) < 2 - p$. Therefore, we have

$$\text{REV} = \frac{1}{2}\left[(2-p)^2 \cdot p + \left(p-1-\frac{q-1}{\delta}\right)\left(1-\frac{q-\delta p}{1-\delta}\right)q\right]$$

$$\leqslant \frac{1}{2}\left[(2-p)^2 \cdot p + \left(p-1-\frac{q-1}{1}\right) \cdot (2-p) \cdot q\right]$$

$$= \left(p-\frac{1}{2}\right)\left[-\frac{3}{4}p^2 + 2p - \left(q-\frac{p}{2}\right)^2\right]$$

Since $p > 1$ and $\frac{p}{2} < 1 < q$, the supremum of REV is achieved when $q = 1$ (though $q \in (1, 2]$). Thus,

$$\text{REV} < \left(p-\frac{1}{2}\right)\left[-\frac{3}{4}p^2 + 2p - \left(1-\frac{p}{2}\right)^2\right] = \frac{1}{2}\left(p^3 - 5p^2 + 7p - 2\right)$$

According to the first order condition, the local maximum and local minimum of the right-hand-side is reached when $p = 1$ and $p = \frac{7}{3}$, respectively. In other words, the supremum of REV is when $p = 1$ even though $p \in (1, 2]$:

$$\text{REV} < \frac{1}{2}\left(1^3 - 5 \cdot 1^2 + 7 \cdot 1 - 2\right) = \frac{1}{2} < \frac{59}{108}$$

Now we present the proof of Theorem 2.2 based on the above results.

Proof (Proof of Theorem 2.2)　By Lemma 2.3, we fix $\alpha = 1$ and $\beta = 1$. Moreover, without loss of generality, we could focus on the cases where $p > q$. Otherwise, the menu entry B will be dominated by A

and Z, i.e., $S_B = \varnothing$, hence reduced a menu with at most 2 entries, where the optimal revenue is at most $\dfrac{2\sqrt{6}}{9}$.

Similarly, by Lemma 2.4, we fix, without loss of generality, $\gamma = 1$. Otherwise, if $(\gamma, \delta) = (0, 0)$, the menu entry B is dominated by Z, again reduced to a menu with at most 2 entries.

Therefore, it remains to solve the program (3Menu) with additional constraints: $\alpha = \beta = \gamma = 1$ and $p > q$. Now consider the values $v = (v_1, v_2)$ in $S_A \cap S_B$,

$$S_A \cap S_B = \{v \mid (v_1, v_2) \cdot (1, 1) - p = (v_1, v_2) \cdot (1, \delta) - q\}$$

Similarly,

$$S_A \cap S_Z = \{v \mid (v_1, v_2) \cdot (1, 1) = p\},$$

$$S_B \cap S_Z = \{v \mid (v_1, v_2) \cdot (1, \delta) = q\}$$

and hence

$$S_A \cap S_B \cap S_Z = \left\{ (v_1^*, v_2^*) \;\middle|\; v_1^* = \frac{q - \delta p}{1 - \delta},\, v_2^* = \frac{p - q}{1 - \delta} \right\}$$

Note that if S_A or S_B is empty, there would be only two menu entries and the revenue cannot be more than $\dfrac{2\sqrt{6}}{9}$. Otherwise:

- If S_A is not empty, we must have $v_2^* < 1$, hence $\dfrac{p - q}{1 - \delta} < 1$;

- If S_B is not empty, we must have $v_1^* < 1$, hence $\dfrac{q - \delta p}{1 - \delta} < 1$.

Based on these constraints, there are three possible cases (see Figure 2.11). According to Lemma 2.5, 2.6 and 2.7, the optimal menu with at most 3 entries is to sell the first item at price $\dfrac{2}{3}$ or the bundle of two items at price $\dfrac{5}{6}$, yielding revenue $\dfrac{59}{108}$.

2.3 Performance

As our method is very efficient, we are able to perform our experiments using TensorFlow on a laptop with a 2.5 GHz Intel Core i7 CPU and 16 GB of RAM. To solve the problems with continuous value distributions, we simply discretize the value space with parameter N, which is the number of the intervals (with length $1/N$) in unit length. In other words, there are N^2 squares of size $1/N$ by $1/N$ in any unit square. By default, we set $N = 100$.

We compare the running time of our MENUNET and the linear program approach for the $U[0,1]^2$ setting. To solve the linear program, we also need to discretize the value space. Let $f(v)$ be the probability that the buyer's value is v. The variables of the linear program are the allocation $x = (x_1, x_2)$ and payment p for each value (hence $O(N^2)$ variables) and the constraints are the IC and IR constraints (hence $O(N^4)$ constraints).

$$\max \quad \sum_{v \in V} f(v)p(v)$$

$$\text{s.t.} \quad v^T x(v) - p(v) \geqslant 0, \forall v \in V$$

$$v^T x(v) - p(v) \geqslant v^T x(v') - p(v'), \forall v, v' \in V$$

$$0 \leqslant x(v) \leqslant 1, \forall v \in V$$

We use the basic PuLP package in Python to solve the linear programs. In Figure 2.12(a), we compare the execution time of solving the linear programs with specific N's ($N = 10, 15, 20, 25, 30$) and the execution time of training our neural network to (i) achieve a mechanism with at least the same level of accuracy as the one given by the linear program (for $N \leqslant 30$), and (ii) converge (for $N = 40, 50, 200$). Note that the running time of the linear program approach grows very rapidly: for $N = 30$, it takes 51 minutes and we are not able to apply it to any $N \geqslant 40$, since it takes too long for the solver to find a solution. In contrast, the training time of our neural network grows much slower (less than 5 minutes for $N = 200$, i.e., buyer distribution support of size 40000).

One key advantage of our approach over the linear program is that our problem size grows linearly in terms of the support size of the buyer's value distribution (i.e., $O(N^2)$), while the size of the linear program grows much faster in terms of the support size (i.e., $O(N^4)$). In Figure 2.12(b), we also plot the average training time for each iteration, which ranges from 1 to roughly 28 milliseconds.

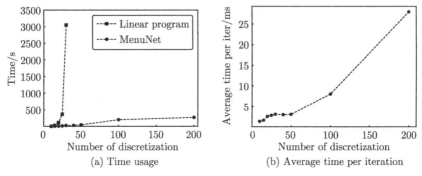

(a) Time usage   (b) Average time per iteration

Figure 2.12　Running time and convergence speed

To describe how close a mechanism is to the theoretically optimal one, we define the *relative optimality* to be the ratio between the revenue generated by the mechanism and that generated by the optimal one: $\frac{\text{REV}}{\text{OPTREV}}$, where OPTREV is the revenue of the optimal mechanism in theory. REV is evaluated on the original value distribution, rather than using the value produced by the loss function of the network. Figure 2.13 shows that our method converges to the optimal quickly. The gap between REV and OPTREV can not drop to zero as we discretized the value distribution.

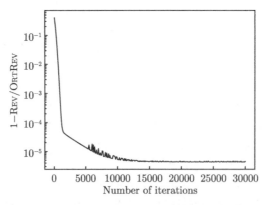

Figure 2.13　Relative optimality (smoothed)

Figure 2.14, Figure 2.15 and Figure 2.16 show that our method is also better than the linear programming method in terms of accuracy. Recall that the black lines inside the area are drawn according to the theoretically optimal solution. Table 2.1 summarizes the accuracy of our method in different settings and N is set to 100.

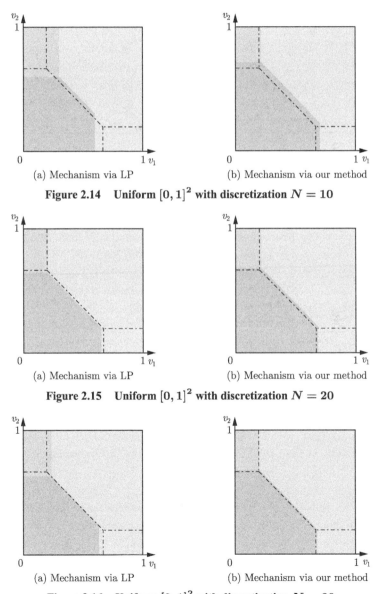

(a) Mechanism via LP

(b) Mechanism via our method

Figure 2.14   Uniform $[0, 1]^2$ with discretization $N = 10$

(a) Mechanism via LP

(b) Mechanism via our method

Figure 2.15   Uniform $[0, 1]^2$ with discretization $N = 20$

(a) Mechanism via LP

(b) Mechanism via our method

Figure 2.16   Uniform $[0, 1]^2$ with discretization $N = 30$

Table 2.1　Comparison with optimal mechanisms, where the actual revenue is not given by the loss of the network, but computed based on the original value distribution and the menu given by our networks

Distributions	Actual REV	Optimal REV	REV/OPTREV
$U[0,1]^2$	0.5491989	$(12+2\sqrt{2})/27$	$\geqslant 99.9996\%$
$U[0,1] \times [0,1.5]$	0.6838542	$(15+2\sqrt{3})/27$	$\geqslant 99.9997\%$
$U[0,1] \times [0,1.9]$	0.7888323	$(17.4+2\sqrt{3.8})/27$	$\geqslant 99.9988\%$
$U[0,1] \times [0,2]$	0.8148131	$22/27$	$\geqslant 99.9997\%$
$U[0,1] \times [0,2.5]$	0.9435182	$1019/1080$	$\geqslant 99.99996\%$
$U[0,1]^2$ menu size $\leqslant 3$	0.5462947	$59/108$	$\geqslant 99.9997\%$
$U[0,1]^2$ menu size $\leqslant 2$	0.5443309	$2\sqrt{6}/9$	$\geqslant 99.99997\%$
$U\{v_1,v_2 \geqslant 0 | v_1/2 + v_2 \leqslant 1\}$	0.5491225	$(12+2\sqrt{2})/27$	$\geqslant 99.9857\%$

References

[1] SHEN W, TANG P, ZUO S. Automated mechanism design via neural networks[C]//Proceedings of the 18th International Joint Conference on Autonomous Agents and Multi-agent Systems. AAMAS, 2019, 1: 215-223.

[2] CONITZER V, SANDHOLM T. Complexity of mechanism design[C]// Proceedings of the 18th Conference on Uncertainty in Artificial Intelligence. Morgan Kaufmann Publishers Inc., 2002: 103-110.

[3] HARTLINE J D, ROUGHGARDEN T. Simple versus optimal mechanisms[C]//Proceedings of the 10th of ACM Conference on Electronic Commerce. ACM, 2009: 225-234.

[4] HART S, NISAN N. Approximate revenue maximization with multiple items[J]. Journal of Economic Theory, 2017, 172: 313-347.

[5] CAI Y, DASKALAKIS C, WEINBERG S M. An algorithmic characterization of multi-dimensional mechanism[C]//Proceedings of the 44th Annual ACM Symposium on Theory of Computing. ACM, 2012: 459-478.

[6] CAI Y, DASKALAKIS C, WEINBERG S M. Optimal multi-dimensional mechanism design: Reducing revenue to welfare maximization[C]//IEEE 53rd Annual Symposium on Foundations of Computer Science. IEEE, 2012: 130-139.

[7] LI X, YAO ACC. On revenue maximization for selling multiple independently distributed items[C]//Proceedings of the National Academy of Sciences, 2013: 110(28): 11232-11237.

[8]   YAO ACC. An n-to-1 bidder reduction for multi-item auctions and its applications[C]//Proceedings of 2015 ACM-SIAM Symposium on Discrete Algorithms. Society for Industrial and Applied Mathematics, 2015: 92-109.

[9]   SANDHOLM T, LIKHODEDOV A. Automated design of revenue-maximizing combinatorial auctions[J]. Operations Research: The Journal of the Operations Research Society of America, 2015, 63(5): 1000-1025.

[10] YAO ACC. On solutions for the maximum revenue multi-item auction under dominant-strategy and Bayesian implementations[P]. 10.48550/arXiv.1607.03685. 2016.

[11] TANG P, WANG Z. Optimal auctions for negatively correlated items[C]//Proceedings of the 2016 ACM Conference on Economics and Computation. ACM, 2016: 103-120.

[12] TANG P, WANG Z. Optimal mechanisms with simple menus[J]. Journal of Mathematical Economics, 2017, 69: 54-70.

[13] ARMSTRONG M. Multiproduct nonlinear pricing[J]. Econometrica-.Journal of the Econometric Society, 64(1): 51-75.

[14] MANELLI A M, VINCENT D R. Multidimensional mechanism design: Revenue maximization and the multiple-good monopoly[J]. Journal of Economic Theory 137(1): 153-185

[15] PAVLOV G. Optimal mechanism for selling two goods[J]. The BE Journal of Theoretical Economics, 2011: 11(1).

[16] DASKALAKIS C, DECKELBAUM A, TZAMOS C. Mechanism design via optimal transport[C]//Proceedings of the 14th ACM Conference on Electronic Commerce. ACM, 2013: 269-286.

[17] ALESI S, FU H, HAGHPANAH N, et al. Bayesian optimal auctions via multi-to single-agent reduction[C]//Proceedings of the 13th ACM Conference on Electronic Commerce. ACM, 2012: 17-17.

[18] CARROLL G. Robustness and Separation in Multidimensional Screening[J]. Econometrica, 2017, 85(2): 453-488.

[19] DÜTTING P, FENG Z, NARASIMHAN H, et al. Optimal auctions through deep learning[C]//Proceedings of the 36th International Conference on Machine Learning, 2019.

[20] VOHRA R V. Mechanism design: a linear programming approach[M]. Cambridge University Press, 2011.

[21] RUBINSTEIN A. Modeling bounded rationality[J]. Southern Economic Journal, 1998, 1(:n2): 366-368.

[22] GIGERENZER G, SELTEN R. Bounded rationality: The adaptive toolbox[J]. Psychology and Marketing, 2003, 20(1): 87-92.

[23] TANG P, SANDHOLM T. Optimal auctions for spiteful bidders[C]// Proceedings of the 26th AAAI Conference on Artificial Intelligence. AAAI, 2012: 1457-1463.

[24] WANG Z, TANG P. Optimal auctions for partially rational bidders[C]// Proceedings of the 24th International Conference on Artificial Intelligence. AAAI, 2015: 118-124.

[25] THIRUMULANATHAN D, SUNDATESAN R, NARAHARI Y. Optimal mechanism for selling two items to a single buyer having uniformly distributed valuations[C]//International Conference on Web and Internet Economics. Springer Berlin Heidelberg, 2016: 174-187.

[26] THIRUMULANATHAN D, SUNDATESAN R, NARAHARI Y. On optimal mechanisms in the two-item single-buyer unit-demand setting[J]. Journal of Mathematical Economics, 2019, 82: 31-60.

[27] DÜTTING P, FENG Z, NARASIMHAN H, et al. Optimal auctions through deep learning[J]. 2017.

[28] DASKALAKIS C.Multi-item auctions defying intuition?[C]//ACM SIGecom Exchanges, 2015, 14(1): 41-75.

[29] PAVLOV G.A property of solutions to linear monopoly problems[J].The BEJournal of Theoretical Economics, 2011, 11(1): 395-398.

Chapter 3   Dynamic Mechanism Design via AI-Driven Approaches

In the standard mechanism design model, the seller has a single item for sale and the buyers participate in the mechanism in a one-shot fashion. In real-world applications such as online advertising, the platform has multiple items (impressions) that are sold to the buyers in a repeated fashion. However, in the repeated setting, the buyers' action space may grow exponentially with respect to the number of auction rounds. Thus they may have much more complicated preferences and strategies. Similarly, the design space of the mechanisms is also significantly larger than in the one-shot setting. Such large spaces pose serious challenges in designing mechanisms with desirable performances.

In this chapter, we explore how AI approaches can be applied to overcome the above difficulties. We consider two different settings, both motivated by online ad auctions. In the first setting (Section 3.1), we aim to design the so-called *cost-per-action* (CPA) auctions, where each advertiser only needs to pay after the user has done specific actions (e.g., purchases) in the advertiser's website. Compared to *cost-per-click* (CPC) auctions, the CPA auctions eliminate the uncertainty faced by the advertisers. Moreover, we require the mechanism to be ex-post individually rational, making the mechanism more performance-oriented. Inspired by algorithms in the "multi-armed bandit" literature and the so-called "bank account" mechanism in repeated auctions, we design a "credit" mechanism, and also provide an economic interpretation. With the combination of the AI approach and the economic interpretation, our mechanism is easy to implement and has desirable guarantees.

In the second setting (Section 3.2), we aim to tackle the so-called "second-order effect" in online ad auctions, where the advertisers change their strategies in reaction to new mechanisms. To understand how the advertisers respond, we propose a recurrent neural network-based buyer behavior model and fit the model with a large amount of real auction data. We formulate the dynamic mechanism design problem as a Markov decision process and use reinforcement learning techniques to find a solution. This framework has already been adopted by the major Chinese search engine Baidu, and was highlighted in Baidu's Q1 Financial Report of 2018[1].

3.1　Dynamic Cost-Per-Action Auctions with Ex-Post IR Guarantees[①]

In this section, we consider a repeated auction between one seller and many buyers, where each buyer only has an estimation of his value in each period but does not know its realization until he actually receives the item in that period. This setting is motivated by the online ad auctions. The buyers participate in a dynamic auction but require ex-post IR.

We use a structure that we call *credit accounts* to enable a general reduction from any *IC* and *ex-ante IR* dynamic auction to an *approximate IC* and *ex-post IR* dynamic auction with credit accounts. Our reduction obtains stronger IR guarantees at the cost of a weaker notion of IC. Surprisingly, our reduction works without any common knowledge assumption. Finally, as a complement to our reduction, we prove that there is no non-trivial auction that is exactly IC and ex-post IR under this setting.

3.1.1　Background

Most online advertising platforms, such as search engines and social media, have gone through the evolution from the *cost-per-mille impressions* (CPM) model to the *cost-per-click* (CPC) model, where the

---

① This section was originally published as [2]: Weiran Shen, Zihe Wang, and Song Zuo. Ex-post IR Dynamic Auctions with Cost-per-Action Payments[C]//Proceedings of the 27th International Joint Conference on Artificial Intelligence and the 23rd European Conference on Artificial Intelligence. AAAI Press, 2018: 505-511.

former is aligned with traditional advertising industry while the latter focuses more on performance. In the CPC model, when a user visits a certain web page, the platform collects bids from the advertisers and based on the bids, determines whose ad to display on the page. The corresponding advertiser is charged when his ad is clicked by the user. Such an advertising model is called the CPC model because the advertiser only needs to pay when his ad is clicked. This CPC model has been the de facto model for most major online advertising platforms, and is proven to be profitable[3]. However, despite its success, this model is criticized to have the click fraud problem, i.e., the competitors of an advertiser, or even the platform itself, may deliberately create false clicks to increase the advertiser's cost or to extract more revenue. Furthermore, the advertisers have to pay for clicks that do not lead to final purchases of their products. Although one may argue that in expectation the advertisers are indeed profitable, it may still be a serious problem for small companies that cannot ignore such risks.

A relatively new model that has gained much research attention recently is the *cost-per-action* (CPA) advertising model. In contrast to the CPC model, the CPA model is even more performance-oriented and focuses directly on user actions. In the CPA model, the advertisers are only charged when the users make certain actions, such as purchases or transactions. It seems that the CPA model and the CPC model are almost the same except for the payment. However, this advertising model clears the uncertainty faced by the advertiser and can potentially decrease the vulnerability to click fraud. Besides these advantages, the CPA model also gives more incentives to the platforms to deliver high-quality impressions to the users. In 2007, the CPA model was described as the "Holy Grail" of targeted advertising by Google [4]. Currently, many online advertising platforms, including Google, eBay, Amazon, Facebook, Baidu, and WeChat have already started to test the CPA model.

Another essential difference between these two models is that the platform can not directly observe the users' actions on the advertisers' websites whereas the users' clicks are observable by both the platform and the advertiser. Such an undesirable property may cause the advertisers to hide the users' actions to avoid payments. This also poses challenges in putting the CPA model into practice to replace the CPC model that is currently dominant in the online advertising industry.

Therefore, when compared with the standard buyer model, the buyer model in this setting has two major differences:

- The buyers require ex-post IR instead of interim or ex-ante IR;
- The buyers can also misreport the users' actions besides misreporting their values.

To tackle these problems, we present the *credit account mechanism.* Our mechanism solves the incentive issue by adding a credit account for each advertiser on top of the original mechanism that follows the "allocate-report-pay" scheme. In our mechanism, the advertisers are given a certain amount of "credit quota" and an advertiser can not win the auction if his "credit quota" runs out. When an impression is allocated, the winner observes his value and reports to the platform. The mechanism then charges him according to some modified payment rule based on the original mechanism. The payment is chosen such that it never exceeds the bidder's reported value so that ex-post IR is guaranteed. In the meanwhile, the winner's credit balance is updated dynamically according to the difference between his actual payment and his expected payment in the original mechanism.

Intuitively, the credit account keeps track of the difference between one's actual payments and expected payments. An honest advertiser only has a negligible chance of consuming all his credit, while an advertiser shading his reports will quickly run out of credit and will be blocked in future auctions.

3.1.2　Our Contributions

Firstly, we formalize the credit accounts framework[①]. As for IC and IR properties, our framework can reduce any IC and ex-ante IR mechanism to a credit account mechanism that gives the same allocation rule as the original one with high probability (Theorem 3.1) and guarantees approximate IC (Definition 3.4) and ex-post IR (Definition 3.3). We emphasize that the notion of approximate IC serves as the

---

① In fact, we are not the first to use the idea of credit accounts in mechanism design. Similar reputation-based structures are used for other settings[5-6].

motivating example of online advertising, since the benefit of deviation on average is vanishingly small as the number of periods grows (Theorem 3.2).

Such a reduction then naturally induces the trade-off between the strength of truthfulness and the probability of the desired implementation (see Section 3.1.6). In particular, it also applies to second-price auctions (Corollary 3.1).

Finally, as a complement to the constructed credit account mechanisms, we show that strict IC and ex-post IR can not be achieved simultaneously by any non-trivial mechanisms (Theorem 3.3). In this sense, credit account mechanisms have achieved the strongest properties we can hope for.

3.1.3 Related Works

Ever since Myerson's seminal paper on designing revenue optimal auctions [7], there has been intensive researche on analyzing and designing one-shot auction mechanisms. For example, Edelman et al. [3] and Varian [8] study the performance of the generalized second-price auction (GSP). Hartline and Roughgarden [9], Shen and Tang [10], and Bachrach et al. [11] provide mechanisms that can tradeoff among different objectives. There is also a rich literature on multi-item auctions [12-16], and on repeated auctions motivated by online advertising [17-22].

A closely related topic is dynamic mechanism design (see Bergemann and Välimäki [23] for a comprehensive survey). Our mechanism is also related to works on auctions with unknown types, for example, the "common value" literature [24-25].

There is also a series of works that focus on designing mechanisms with the CPA advertising model. Nazerzadeh et al. [26] study the setting where the advertisers' values may evolve over time. Based on multi-armed bandit algorithms, they present a mechanism that satisfies asymptotic IR and asymptotic IC. However, their mechanism does not exactly fall into the CPA advertising model, since the winner still needs to pay even if the user does not click on the ad. Hu et al. [27] compare the CPC model and the CPA model. Their results show that the CPA model is better in incentivizing the platform to improve the purchase rate, but suffers from the adverse selection problem. Agarwal et al.[28] consider a similar setting where the advertisers report both the predefined actions and the action probabilities. They show that at equilibrium, the advertisers may report skewed bids. However, their results only hold in one-shot games.

Our mechanism also borrows some high-level ideas from the so-called "bank account" mechanism, where the seller maintains a "bank account" for each buyer during the dynamic auction [29-32]. Although with similar names, the "credit account" here is fundamentally different: (i) the bank account mechanisms are designed under the common knowledge assumption to ensure dynamic IC, while our credit account mechanism guarantees approximate dynamic IC *without* any common knowledge assumptions; (ii) the "balance" in a bank account can be thought of as money, and the buyers can pay the seller with the bank account balance, while the "credit" in the credit account is more like a reliability measure of the buyers based on their past behaviors.

3.1.4 Setting and Preliminaries

We study the problem of designing cost-per-action mechanisms in an environment with one seller and multiple buyers. In particular, we will focus on the setting with repeated sales, that is, in each period, the seller has a new item to sell to the buyers. If not sold, the item is then destroyed immediately. We consider the finite horizon case without discount factor, hence $T < \infty$①. For simplicity, we will use $[T] = \{1, 2, \cdots, T\}$ and $[n] = \{1, 2, \cdots, n\}$ to denote the set of time horizon and the set of agents, respectively.

Similar to the standard setting, in each period, what the seller does is to allocate the item to at most one of the buyers and charge the buyers some amount of money as payments. Formally, we use $x_i^t \in [0, 1]$ to denote the probability of buyer $i \in [n]$ receiving the item in period t and $p_i^t \in \mathbb{R}$ to denote the payment from buyer i to the seller in period t.

The main difference between our setting and the standard setting is how the buyers value the received items:

- In the standard setting, each buyer i has a private value v_i^t of the

---

① The extension to infinite horizon case with discount factor is straightforward.

t-th item, and v_i^t is known to buyer i before the t-th auction[①];

- In our setup, each buyer is uncertain about his value for the item until he actually receives it.

Formally, an *estimation* of buyer i for the t-th item is a private distribution F_i^t of his possible *exact values* (v_i^t follows distribution F_i^t), and his *exact value* $v_i^t \in [0, \bar{v}]$ is realized only after receiving the item[②]. We assume that the value profile $v^t = (v_1^t, v_2^t, \cdots, v_n^t)$ of time t is sampled from the joint distribution F^t but is independent over time. Hence F_i^t is a marginal distribution of F^t for buyer i. We also allow each F_i^t to be different across both the buyers and periods.

Although such a setting is quite different from the canonical auction setting, it does help us to capture the nature of online advertising. In online advertising, there are two types of ads, brand-based ads and performance-based ads. For the first type of ads, the advertisers gain utility whenever the ads are shown to a user, while for the second type of ad, the advertisers gain utility from some specific user actions on their websites (e.g., buying some goods or services, subscribing to the website). In other words, for the second type of ads, the advertisers only have estimations of their values for an impression (or a click) to a user, while his exact value depends on the actual actions taken by the user.

Under such a setting, we assume that both estimation F_i^t and the exact value v_i^t are the private information of buyer i. Although in general, the estimation could rely on both the seller's private information, such as the characteristics of the user, and the buyer's private information, such as the prior knowledge of certain users' behaviors. However, such an information structure is not our main focus. Hence, to make the model clean, we assume that the estimation F_i^t is private information of buyer i. With such a simplification, we can ensure a more robust incentive guarantee for the buyers. In fact, our results can also be easily extended to more general settings.

Throughout this section, we focus on "direct mechanisms", where the seller requires the buyers to report all their private information and

---

① In Bayesian settings, the other agents (including the seller and the other buyers) might only have knowledge of the distribution of v_i^t.

② $\bar{v}$ is just a finite upper bound on the buyer's value and does not restrict the bid of the buyers (see Mechanism 3.1).

determine the allocation of the item and the payments from the buyers. Although in general, reporting the entire estimation F_i^t is required, for most practical mechanisms, reporting the expected value $E[F_i^t]$ would suffice.

The following abstract auction outlines the common structure of a direct mechanism under this setup.

Mechanism 3.1 (Abstract direct mechanism) *For each period* $t \in [T]$*:*

1. Each buyer has a private estimation F_i^t for the t-th item and reports an estimation $\hat{F}_i^t$ to the seller;

2. The seller determines the allocation $x^t \in [0,1]^n$ of the t-th item based on the reported estimations $\hat{F}^t$ and all the historical reports $\hat{F}^{1:t-1}$ and $\hat{v}^{1:t-1}$, where we define

$$\hat{F}^{1:t-1} = \hat{F}^1, \hat{F}^2, \cdots, \hat{F}^{t-1} \quad and \quad \hat{v}^{1:t-1} = \hat{v}^1, \hat{v}^2, \cdots, \hat{v}^{t-1}$$

3. The winner j receives the item, realizes his exact value $v_j^t \sim F_j^t$, and reports $\hat{v}_j^t \in \mathbb{R}_+$ to the seller;

4. The seller determines the payment $p^t = (p_1^t, p_2^t, \cdots, p_n^t)$ based on the reported estimations and values from the current and past periods, i.e., $\hat{F}^{1:t}, \hat{v}^{1:t}$.

Before we proceed, we need to redefine some terms in this repeated context. Since only the winner reports his exact value at the end of each period, hence v^t (or $\hat{v}^t$) is a vector consisting of one $v_{j_t}^t$ (or $\hat{v}_{j_t}^t$) and $n-1$ empty elements $\perp$:

$$v^t = (\perp, \cdots, v_{j_t}^t, \cdots, \perp) \quad and \quad \hat{v}^t = (\perp, \cdots, \hat{v}_{j_t}^t, \cdots, \perp)$$

where j_t is the index of the winner in period $t^{①}$. We assume that each buyer has a quasi-linear utility. But now both the allocation x_i^t and the payment p_i^t depend on the buyers' reported history.

$$u_i^t(\hat{F}^{1:t}, \hat{v}^{1:t}; v_i^t) = v_i^t \cdot x_i^t(\hat{F}^{1:t}, \hat{v}^{1:t-1}) - p_i^t(\hat{F}^{1:t}, \hat{v}^{1:t})$$

His cumulative utility is the sum of his utility over all time periods:

$$U_i(\hat{F}^{1:T}, \hat{v}^{1:T}; v_i^{1:T}) = \sum_{t \in [T]} u_i^t(\hat{F}^{1:t}, \hat{v}^{1:t}; v_i^t)$$

---

① If there is no winner in period t, then $v^t = \hat{v}^t = (\perp, \cdots, \perp)$.

Finally, we define the revenue of the seller REV, and the social welfare of the mechanism WEL:

$$\text{REV} = \sum_{t\in[T]}\sum_{i\in[n]} p_i^t, \quad \text{WEL} = \sum_{t\in[T]}\sum_{i\in[n]} v_i^t \cdot x_i^t = \text{REV} + \sum_{i\in[n]} U_i$$

We assume the buyers are risk-neutral and self-interested, hence the best strategy of each buyer i must maximize his cumulative utility U_i. We do not set any specific goal for the seller now, since we mainly focus on the implementation. A direct mechanism is *dominant-strategy truthful* or *dominant-strategy incentive compatible*, if in each period t, reporting $\hat{F}_i^t = F_i^t$ and $\hat{v}_i^t = v_i^t$ (if he won the item) is the dominant strategy of buyer i, regardless of the strategies of others and all historical reports. In this section, we focus on dominant-strategy IC because we do not make any common knowledge assumptions.

Let $\langle \hat{F}^{1:t}, \hat{v}^{1:t} \rangle$ be any reporting profile, and $\langle \hat{F}_{*i\tau}^{1:t}, \hat{v}_{*i\tau}^{1:t} \rangle$ be the reporting profile where buyer i reports truthfully in periods $\tau, \cdots, t$, while the other entries remain the same:

$$\hat{F}_{*i\tau}^{1:t} = (\hat{F}^{1:\tau-1}, \hat{F}_{-i}^{\tau:t}, F_i^{\tau:t}),$$

$$\hat{v}_{*i\tau}^{1:t} = (\hat{v}^{1:\tau-1}, \hat{v}_{-i}^{\tau:t}, v_i^{\tau:t})$$

where $-i$ indicates the quantities for all buyers other than i.

For ease of presentation, we define the following notations. Let I_{it} be the expected utility of buyer i reporting both his estimation and actual value truthfully since period t with arbitrary fixed historical reports:

$$\mathrm{I}_{it} = \mathrm{E}_{v_i^{t:T} \sim F_i^{t:T}} \left[U_i(\hat{F}_{*it}^{1:T}, \hat{v}_{*it}^{1:T}; v_i^{1:T}) \right]$$

And let II_{it} be the utility of buyer i reporting his actual value truthfully since period t, but reporting his estimation truthfully since period $t+1$:

$$\mathrm{II}_{it} = \mathrm{E}_{v_i^{t:T} \sim F_i^{t:T}} \left[U_i(\hat{F}_{*i,t+1}^{1:T}, \hat{v}_{*it}^{1:T}; v_i^{1:T}) \right]$$

We define I_{it}' and II_{it}' similarly:

$$\mathrm{I}_{it}' = \mathrm{E}_{v_i^{t+1:T} \sim F_i^{t+1:T}} \left[U_i(\hat{F}_{*i,t+1}^{1:T}, \hat{v}_{*it}^{1:T}; v_i^{1:T}) \right],$$

$$\text{II}'_{it} = \text{E}_{v_i^{t+1:T} \sim F_i^{t+1:T}} \left[U_i(\hat{F}_{*i,t+1}^{1:T}, \hat{v}_{*i,t+1}^{1:T}; v_i^{1:T}) \right]$$

Formally, we have the following definitions:

Definition 3.1 ((Dynamic) Dominant-strategy incentive compatibility) A direct mechanism is dominant-strategy incentive compatible, if truthfully reporting is the best strategy for each buyer i in each period t (both before and after the allocation of the item):

$$\begin{cases} \text{I}_{it} \geqslant \text{I}'_{it}, & \forall i, t, \hat{F}^{1:T}, \hat{v}^{1:T}, F_i^{1:T}, v_i^{1:t-1} \\ \text{II}_{it} \geqslant \text{II}'_{it}, & \forall i, t, \hat{F}^{1:T}, \hat{v}^{1:T}, F_i^{1:T}, v_i^{1:t} \end{cases} \tag{DIC}$$

Definition 3.2 (Ex-ante individual rationality) A direct mechanism is ex-ante individually rational, if each buyer's *expected* utility in each period t is non-negative:

$$\text{E}_{v_i^t \sim F_i^t} \left[u_i^t(\hat{F}_{*it}^{1:t}, \hat{v}_{*it}^{1:t}; v_i^t) \right] \geqslant 0, \quad \forall \hat{F}_{*it}^{1:t}, \hat{v}^{1:t} \tag{Ex-ante IR}$$

Similarly, we can define ex-post individual rationality:

Definition 3.3 (Ex-post individual rationality) A direct mechanism is ex-post individual rational, if for any buyer i, his utility u_i^t in each period t for any v_i^t is non-negative:

$$u_i^t(\hat{F}_{*it}^{1:t}, \hat{v}_{*it}^{1:t}; v_i^t) \geqslant 0, \quad \forall i, t, \hat{F}_{*it}^{1:t}, \hat{v}_{*it}^{1:t} \tag{Ex-post IR}$$

We briefly describe two auction formats widely studied for real applications, i.e., *cost-per-action* (a.k.a. pay-per-action) auctions and *cost-per-click* (a.k.a. pay-per-click) auctions. In addition, we also compare their advantages and disadvantages, which in turn motivate us to combine their advantages.

Cost-per-action auctions. In CPA auctions, advertisers bid for users' specific actions on their websites and will only be charged when the users' actually performed these actions. One important technical issue is that, unlike the clicks on the seller's website, these actions are performed on the adversiters' websites, and are not directly observed by the seller. So the advertisers need to report them to the seller. But they may misreport the actions to avoid paying the seller. Even if the seller requires the advertisers to install certain software so that these actions could be monitored by the seller, they can still lie via manipulating the software since the potential profits could be significant[28].

Since the drawback might be intolerable for the seller, cost-per-action type auctions are rarely adopted in practice except for some cases where the actions are directly observable by the seller①.

Cost-per-click auctions. In CPC auctions, advertisers bid for user clicks on their ads displayed on the seller's website, which can be directly observed by both the seller and the corresponding advertiser. However, for many advertisers, the clicks do not directly generate utility for them — their utilities come from the potential user actions after the clicks. In other words, given the ad being clicked, the utility of the advertiser is a random variable depending on the potential user actions. Even when the user does not do anything on their website, the advertiser still needs to pay the same amount of money for this click. In practice, the probability of user action conditional on being clicked could be relatively small. Hence the variance of such random variables could be high and causes high-risk cost for the advertisers. Even worse, their cumulative utility might be negative with a certain probability in theory.

The cost-per-click auction satisfies ex-ante IR but does not satisfy ex-post IR, hence the buyer utility incurs a risk of being negative. Such a risk is not desirable, which makes the system less robust and in the long term would eventually lead to a loss in the seller's revenue. However, it is much more tolerable compared with the risk of the revenue loss in cost-per-action auctions. This is, in fact, a major reason why cost-per-click auctions instead of cost-per-action auctions are adopted in most of the environments in online advertising, where the user actions are only privately observable to the advertisers.

Despite the potential revenue loss faced by cost-per-action auctions, it still has many other properties that are more desirable than cost-per-click auctions[33].

---

① For example, when the advertiser bids on Google's platform for his apps on Google Play, the seller, Google, can easily monitor the actions of downloading or installing the apps by the users. This is also called the cost-per-install (or pay-per-install) model. See https://en.wikipedia.org/wiki/Compensation_methods\#Pay-per-install_(PPI).

3.1.5　Mechanisms

In this section, we first discuss several AI techniques that are useful in solving the problems in CPA auctions. However, it is still not clear how to solve these problems completely by applying these approaches. We then provide an economic interpretation (credit account) of these AI approaches. With such an interpretation, we are able to reduce any dominant-strategy IC and ex-ante IR mechanism to a mechanism that achieves approximate IC (to be defined later) and ex-post IR. Also, the analysis of the resulting mechanism becomes quite easy, although the analysis still borrows ideas from the AI approaches. In particular, as we will show in the next section, the new mechanism implements the same allocation rule as the original one with a high probability when the buyers report truthfully.

3.1.5.1　An Efficient Auction with Ex-Ante IR

Let's start with a simple welfare-maximizing auction that is dominant-strategy IC and ex-ante IR. Then we show how we can strengthen the IR from ex-ante IR to ex-post IR with a tolerable cost in terms of a weaker notion of IC.

Mechanism 3.2 (Ex-ante IR Auction) *In each time period* $t \in [T]$:

1. Ask each buyer to report $\hat{F}_i^t$ *and define his bid as*

$$b_i^t = \mathrm{E}[\hat{F}_i^t] := \mathrm{E}_{v \sim \hat{F}_i^t}[v]$$

or equivalently, ask each buyer to report b_i^t *directly.*

2. Allocate the item to the buyer with the highest bid, break ties arbitrarily:

$$x_i^t = \begin{cases} 1, & \forall j \neq i,\ b_i^t > b_j^t \\ 0, & \exists j \neq i,\ b_i^t < b_j^t \\ \text{break ties arbitrarily}, & \text{otherwise} \end{cases}$$

3. Ignore the winner i's *exact value and simply charge him the second highest bid:*

$$p_i^t = x_i^t \cdot b_{(2)}^t$$

Mechanism 3.2 in each period is actually a second price auction with $E[\hat{F}_i^t]$ as each buyer's bid b_i^t. Note that the payment p_i^t is independent of his reported exact value $\hat{v}_i^t$, so the mechanism dominant-strategy IC. On the other hand, since only the winner is charged, and for each winner,

$$\mathbb{E}_{v_i^t \sim F_i^t}\left[u_i^t\right] = x_i^t \cdot (b_i^t - b_{(2)}^t) \geqslant 0$$

where $b_{(2)}^t = \max_{j \neq i} b_j^t$ is the second highest bid. The mechanism is also ex-ante IR. However, in general, it is not ex-post IR since if buyer j wins in period t and $v_j^t = 0$, $u_j^t = -b_{(2)}^t$ is negative. Therefore, we have:

Lemma 3.1 *Mechanism 3.2 maximizes the social welfare and is dominant-strategy IC and ex-ante IR, but is not ex-post IR.*

3.1.5.2 MAB Algorithms and Economic Interpretations

To guarantee IC, one possible way is to apply Mechanism 3.2. If the buyers' estimations F^t do not change too much over time, the buyer with the highest $E[F_i^t]$ approximately stays the same. Therefore, we can view the problem of learning the highest expected value as a multi-armed bandit problem, and apply a simple ϵ-greedy algorithm. In fact, this is just the high-level idea of Nazerzadeh et al.[26].

However, bandit algorithms usually consist of two different phases: exploration and exploitation. To take advantage of such a mechanism, the buyers can use different strategies during different phases. To address this issue, we can perform a "consistency check"[34] which depends on a relatively stable expected value, and stop selling items to the buyer if his behaviors are not consistent.

In our setting, we do not restrict how the buyers' value estimations change over time. Therefore, it can be difficult to apply the consistency check trick. Furthermore, even if such a technique can be extended to our setting, it is not clear how to analyze the IC guarantee.

We provide an economic interpretation of the consistency check that inspires our solution. Since the buyers' value estimation does not change too much, an honest buyer should pay roughly the same price during the two phases. In other words, his actual average payment should lie inside a small neighborhood around his expected payment with high probability. Now if we view the difference between his actual payment and expected payment as his "reliability" or "credit", then the credit serves as a consistency indicator.

3.1.5.3 The Credit Account Mechanism

Although it is difficult to apply the multi-armed bandit algorithms and consistency check directly to our setting, it turns out that the credit interpretation still works. In fact, it can be applied to much broader settings in the sense that it reduces any dominant-strategy IC and ex-ante IR mechanism $\mathcal{M}$ to another mechanism $\tilde{\mathcal{M}}$ that is *approximate IC* (see Definition 3.4 below) and ex-post IR. Such a reduction significantly simplifies our analysis of these mechanisms.

Definition 3.4 A direct mechanism is ϵ-IC, if for each buyer i, no strategy could outperform truthfully reporting by a margin larger than ϵ:

$$\mathcal{U}_i \geqslant \mathcal{U}_i' - \epsilon, \quad \forall F_i^{1:T}, v_i^{1:T}, \hat{F}^{1:T}, \hat{v}^{1:T} \qquad \text{(Approx IC)}$$

where

$$\mathcal{U}_i = \mathrm{E}_{v_i^{1:T} \sim F_i^{1:T}}[U_i(F_i^{1:T}, \hat{F}_{-i}^{1:T}, v_i^{1:T}, \hat{v}_{-i}^{1:T}; v_i^{1:T})],$$

$$\mathcal{U}_i' = \mathrm{E}_{v_i^{1:T} \sim F_i^{1:T}}[U_i(\hat{F}^{1:T}, \hat{v}^{1:T}; v_i^{1:T})]$$

are buyer i's expected utility for truth-telling and any other strategy, respectively.

To enforce the ex-post IR constraint, the major challenge is that the winner is incentivized to report his exact value as 0, because his payment will be restricted to 0 by the ex-post IR constraint. In other words, if the strict IC constraint is also enforced, the payment must be always 0 and cannot implement general allocation rules.

The credit account mechanism circumvents the contradiction by slightly relaxing the IC constraint as well as tolerating a small probability that the allocation of the resulting mechanism $\tilde{\mathcal{M}}$ is different from the original $\mathcal{M}$.

The core concept of the reduction framework is a *credit account* for each buyer. As mentioned in Section 3.1.5.2, the credit account keeps track of the difference between the total price the buyer should pay under the rule of the original mechanism $\mathcal{M}$ and the price he actually paid so far in the new mechanism $\tilde{\mathcal{M}}$. Since the draws of each $v_i^t \sim F_i^t$ are independent over time, by the law of large numbers, the magnitude of the credit account balance grows at the order of $\sqrt{t}$ with high probability.

Based on the observation, there are two major changes in the new mechanism compared with the original one:

- The payment rule is modified in a way such that it never exceeds the reported exact value $\hat{v}_i^t$ and the expected payment equals the payment under the original mechanism if the buyer reports his exact value truthfully;

- A gradually growing *credit quota*, q^t, is set for each buyer. Once a buyer's credit balance exceeds the quota, he will be labeled as "unreliable" and will not be able to participate in later auctions. Hence his overall benefit of misreporting is essentially bounded by the quota.

Formally, the credit account mechanism $\tilde{\mathcal{M}} = (\tilde{x}, \tilde{p})$ is defined as follows:

Mechanism 3.3 (Credit Account Mechanism) *Let the credit account of buyer i be c_i^t, and set $c_i^1 = 0$ initially. Let q^t be the quota of buyer i at period t. Given the original mechanism $\mathcal{M} = (x, p)$, for each period t:*

1. Ask each buyer i to report $\hat{F}_i^t$ and define α_i^t as[①]:

$$\alpha_i^t = \frac{\min\{c_i^t + q^t, \mathrm{E}[\hat{F}_i^t]\}}{\mathrm{E}[\hat{F}_i^t]} \tag{3.1}$$

2. Allocate the item according to the following allocation rule

$$\tilde{x}_i^t(\mathbf{c}^t, \hat{F}^t) = \alpha_i^t \cdot x_i^t(\hat{F}^{1:t}, \hat{v}^{1:t-1}) \tag{3.2}$$

3. Ask the winner j to report his exact value $\hat{v}_j^t$ and charge him

$$\tilde{p}_j^t(\mathbf{c}^t, \hat{F}^t, \hat{v}^t) = \frac{\alpha_j^t \cdot \hat{v}_j^t}{\mathrm{E}[\hat{F}_j^t]} \cdot \bar{p}_j^t \tag{3.3}$$

where $\bar{p}_j^t$ is his expected payment under the original mechanism $\mathcal{M}$ with value v' sampled from $\hat{F}_j^t$, i.e., $v' \sim \hat{F}_j^t$:

[①] α_i^t is set in a way that ensures the credit balance of buyer i never exceeds his quota in the worst case.

$$\bar{p}_j^t = \mathrm{E}_{v' \sim \hat{F}_j^t} \left[p_j^t (\hat{F}^{1:t}, \hat{v}^{1:t-1}, \hat{v}_{-j}^t, v') \right] \tag{3.4}$$

where v' is just a sample drawn from his reported estimation $\hat{F}_j^t$;

4. Update the credit account of the winner accordingly:

$$c_j^{t+1} = c_j^t + \tilde{p}_j^t - \alpha_j^t \cdot \bar{p}_j^t \tag{3.5}$$

5. For all other buyers, charge them nothing and keep their credit accounts unchanged:

$$\forall i \neq j, \ \tilde{p}_i^t (c^t, \hat{F}^t, \hat{v}^t) = 0, \quad c_i^{t+1} = c_i^t \tag{3.6}$$

3.1.6 Truthfulness and Implementation

With the above general reduction, we can construct a dynamic cost-per-action auction that is approximate efficient, achieving at least $(1 - \delta)$ fraction of the maximum social welfare, and approximate IC with $\epsilon = 2q^T + \bar{v}$ (see Corollary 3.1).

In this section, we present the second main result of this section, which is how the q^T determines the trade-off between implementation tolerance δ and truthfulness tolerance ϵ.

To establish such a trade-off, we prove some even stronger properties of the credit account mechanisms with any general $\mathcal{M}$ that is dominant-strategy IC and ex-ante IR. Intuitively:

- *Implementation:* The resulting credit account mechanism $\tilde{\mathcal{M}}$ implements the same allocation rule as $\mathcal{M}$ with probability at least $1 - \delta$ (see Theorem 3.1);
- *Truthfulness:* The resulting credit account mechanism $\tilde{\mathcal{M}}$ is ϵ-IC and ex-post IR (see Theorem 3.2).

The trade-off between the failure probability δ and the approximate IC ϵ is roughly as follows:

$$\epsilon \leqslant 4\bar{v}\sqrt{t(\ln t + \ln n + \ln \delta^{-1})}$$

We remark that having ϵ sublinear in t is especially meaningful for the application of online advertising, where the maximum value in each period $\bar{v}$ is typically small, whereas T is usually quite large.

Formally, we have the following theorems but defer the proofs to Section 3.1.6.1:

Theorem 3.1 *For any mechanism $\mathcal{M}$ that is dominant-strategy IC and ex-ante IR, and given any $0 < \delta < 1$, there exists a credit account mechanism $\tilde{\mathcal{M}}$ with quota $q^t \leqslant 2\bar{v}\sqrt{t(\ln t + \ln n + \ln \delta^{-1})}$, such that when all buyers report truthfully, for all possible $F^{1:T}$ and $v^{1:T}$ drawn from $F^{1:T}$, the allocation $\tilde{x}^{1:T}$ is the same as in $\mathcal{M}$ with probability $(1 - \delta)$.*

Theorem 3.2 *For any mechanism $\mathcal{M}$ that is dominant-strategy IC and ex-ante IR, the corresponding credit account mechanism $\tilde{\mathcal{M}}$ defined according to Mechanism 3.3 is both ϵ-IC and ex-post IR, with $\epsilon \leqslant 2q^T + \bar{v} = \tilde{O}(\sqrt{T})$.*

Taking Mechanism 3.2 as $\mathcal{M}$, we get a direct corollary:

Corollary 3.1 *Let $\mathcal{M}$ be Mechanism 3.2. The corresponding credit account mechanism $\tilde{\mathcal{M}}$ is both exp-post IR and ϵ-IC with $\epsilon = 2q^T + \bar{v} = \tilde{O}(\sqrt{T})$. Meanwhile, under truthful reporting, $\tilde{\mathcal{M}}$ can achieve at least $(1 - \delta)$ fraction of the maximum social welfare, where δ can be as small as any polynomial of $1/T$, i.e., $\Omega(T^{-k})$ for any constant k.*

In particular, in each period, each buyer only needs to report his expected value $\mathrm{E}[\hat{F}_i^t]$ (instead of his full estimation) and the winner also needs to report his realized value $\hat{v}_i^t$ to the seller.

Proof (Proof of Theorem 3.1) According to the construction of Mechanism 3.3, the allocation of the constructed $\tilde{\mathcal{M}}$ is almost the same as in $\mathcal{M}$. In particular, if

$$\forall i, t, \ \alpha_i^t = 1 \tag{3.7}$$

the allocations, $x^{1:T}$ and $\tilde{x}^{1:T}$, will be exactly the same. Next, we show that the following holds:

$$\Pr[\forall i, t, \ \alpha_i^t = 1] \geqslant 1 - \delta \tag{3.8}$$

Note that $\alpha_i^t < 1$ only if $c_i^t + q^t \leqslant \mathrm{E}[F_i^t] \leqslant \bar{v}$, hence

$$\Pr[\forall i, t, \ \alpha_i^t = 1] \geqslant \Pr[\forall i, t, \ c_i^t \geqslant \bar{v} - q^t]$$

According to the construction of $\tilde{\mathcal{M}}$, for any i, $\{c_i^t\}_{t=1}^T$ is a martingale. To prove this, it suffices to show $\mathrm{E}[c_i^{t+1}|c_i^t] = c_i^t$. If buyer i is not the winner in period t, then $c_i^{t+1} = c_i^t$. Otherwise, buyer i is the winner and according to Equation (3.5),

$$\mathrm{E}[c_i^{t+1}|c_i^t] = \mathrm{E}[c_i^t + \tilde{p}_i^t - \alpha_i^t \cdot \bar{p}_i^t|c_i^t] = c_i^t + \mathrm{E}[\tilde{p}_i^t - \alpha_i^t \cdot \bar{p}_i^t|c_i^t]$$

Equation (3.3) implies that, for any fixed F_i^t,

$$\mathrm{E}[\tilde{p}_i^t|c_i^t, F_i^t] = \mathrm{E}\left[\frac{\alpha_i^t \cdot v_i^t}{\mathrm{E}[F_i^t]} \cdot \bar{p}_i^t|c_i^t, F_i^t\right]$$

$$=\alpha_i^t \cdot \frac{\mathrm{E}_{v_i^t \sim F_i^t}[v_i^t]}{\mathrm{E}[F_i^t]} \cdot \mathrm{E}[\bar{p}_i^t|c_i^t, F_i^t]$$

$$=\alpha_i^t \cdot \bar{p}_i^t$$

where the second equality is from the independence between v_i^t and the randomness of $\bar{p}_i^t$, and the last equality is from Equation (3.4) ($\bar{p}_i^t$ is fixed once c_i^t and F_i^t are given).

Hence $\mathrm{E}[\tilde{p}_i^t - \alpha_i^t \cdot \bar{p}_i^t|c_i^t] = 0$ and $\mathrm{E}[c_i^{t+1}|c_i^t] = c_i^t$, so $\{c_i^t\}_{t=1}^T$ is a martingale. Note that $|c_i^{t+1} - c_i^t| \leqslant \bar{v}$, then by the Azuma-Hoeffding inequality,

$$\mathrm{Pr}[c_i^t - c_i^0 < \bar{v} - q^t] \leqslant \exp\left(-\frac{(\bar{v} - q^t)^2}{2t\bar{v}^2}\right)$$

Setting $q^t = \bar{v} + \bar{v}\sqrt{2t} \cdot \sqrt{2\ln t + \ln n + 2\ln \pi - \ln 6 + \ln \delta^{-1}} = \tilde{O}(\sqrt{t})$, and applying the union bound, we conclude that[1]

$$\mathrm{Pr}[\exists i, t, \ c_i^t < \bar{v} - q^t] \leqslant \sum_{i\in[n], t\in[T]} \mathrm{Pr}[c_i^t - c_i^0 < \bar{v} - q^t]$$

$$\leqslant n \sum_{t\in[T]} \frac{6}{\pi^2} \cdot \frac{\delta}{nt^2}$$

$$\leqslant \delta \cdot \frac{6}{\pi^2} \sum_{t=1}^{\infty} \frac{1}{t^2}$$

$$= \delta$$

Therefore, we complete the proof:

$$\mathrm{Pr}[\forall i, t, \ \alpha_i^t = 1] \geqslant 1 - \mathrm{Pr}[\exists i, t, \ c_i^t < \bar{v} - q^t] \geqslant 1 - \delta$$

---

[1] The famous Basel problem is used here: $\sum_{n=1}^{+\infty} \frac{1}{n^2} = \frac{\pi^2}{6}$, which was first solved by Euler in 1734.

Proof (Proof of Theorem 3.2) We first prove that $\tilde{\mathcal{M}}$ is ex-post IR. Note that the original mechanism $\mathcal{M}$ is ex-ante IR, thus we have that for the winner j in period t,

$$\bar{p}_j^t = \mathrm{E}_{v_j^t}\left[p_j^t(\hat{F}^{1:t}, \hat{v}^{1:t-1}, \hat{v}_{-j}^t, v_j^t)\right]$$
$$\leqslant \mathrm{E}_{v_j^t}\left[v_j^t \cdot x_j^t(\hat{F}^{1:t}, \hat{v}^{1:t-1})\right]$$
$$\leqslant \mathrm{E}[F_j^t] \cdot x_j^t(\hat{F}^{1:t}, \hat{v}^{1:t-1})$$

Then by Equation (3.3),

$$\tilde{p}_j^t = \frac{\alpha_j^t \cdot \hat{v}_j^t}{\mathrm{E}[F_j^t]} \cdot \bar{p}_j^t \leqslant \alpha_j^t \cdot x_j^t \cdot \hat{v}_j^t = \hat{v}_j^t \cdot \tilde{x}_j^t$$

which leads to Equation (Ex-post IR). In particular, for $i \neq j$, the payment is $\tilde{p}_i^t = 0$ according to Equation (3.6), hence (Ex-post IR) holds.

Next, we prove that $\tilde{\mathcal{M}}$ is approximate incentive compatible (Approx IC). We first upper bound one's expected cumulative utility under $\tilde{\mathcal{M}}$.

One key observation is that in Mechanism 3.3, for each buyer i and any fixed $\hat{F}_{-i}^{1:T}$, $\hat{v}_{-i}^{1:T}$ and $F_i^{1:T}$, even if buyer i uses the best strategy in $\tilde{\mathcal{M}}$, his expected cumulative utility $\mathrm{E}[\tilde{U}_i^*]$ under the credit account mechanism $\tilde{\mathcal{M}}$ cannot be much larger than that under the original mechanism $\mathcal{M}$ when using the same strategy:

$$\mathrm{E}[\tilde{U}_i^*] \leqslant \mathrm{E}[U_i^*] + q^T \tag{3.9}$$

To prove this, note that by Equation (3.5) and Equation (3.6), the cumulative payment of each buyer under $\tilde{\mathcal{M}}$ should be close to that under $\mathcal{M}$:

$$\sum_{t\in[T]} \tilde{p}_i^t = c_i^{T+1} + \sum_{t\in[T]} \alpha_i^t \cdot \bar{p}_i^t$$

In the meanwhile, the credit account mechanism, in fact, guarantees that $c_i^{t+1} + q^t \geqslant 0$. Because according to Equation (3.5), we have

$$c_i^{t+1} = c_i^t + \tilde{p}_i^t - \alpha_i^t \cdot \bar{p}_i^t \geqslant c_i^t - \alpha_i^t \cdot \mathrm{E}[\hat{F}_i^t] \geqslant c_i^t - (c_i^t + q^t) = -q^t$$

where the last inequality is from Equation (3.1) that $\alpha_i^t \cdot E[\hat{F}_i^t] = \min\{c_i^t + q^t, E[\hat{F}_i^t]\}$. Therefore, we have

$$\sum_{t \in [T]} \bar{p}_i^t = c_i^{T+1} + \sum_{t \in [T]} \alpha_i^t \cdot \bar{p}_i^t \geqslant -q^T + \sum_{t \in [T]} \alpha_i^t \cdot \bar{p}_i^t$$

Then the expected cumulative utility $E[\tilde{U}_i^*]$ of buyer i under $\tilde{\mathcal{M}}$ can be bounded as follows:

$$E[\tilde{U}_i^*] = E\left[\sum_{t \in [T]} v_i^t \cdot \tilde{x}_i^t - \tilde{p}_i^t\right]$$

$$\leqslant E\left[\sum_{t \in [T]} \alpha_i^t \cdot v_i^t \cdot x_i^t - \alpha_i^t \cdot \bar{p}_i^t\right] + q^T$$

$$= \sum_{t \in [T]} E\left[\alpha_i^t(v_i^t \cdot x_i^t - \bar{p}_i^t)\right] + q^T$$

$$= \sum_{t \in [T]} E\left[\alpha_i^t E_{v_i^t}[v_i^t \cdot x_i^t - \bar{p}_i^t]\right] + q^T$$

where the last equation is because α_i^t, x_i^t, and $\bar{p}_i^t$ are all independent of v_i^t. In particular, since $\mathcal{M}$ is ex-ante IR, we have $E_{v_i^t}[v_i^t \cdot x_i^t - \bar{p}_i^t] \geqslant 0$. Combining that with $\alpha_i^t \leqslant 1$, we have

$$E[\tilde{U}_i^*] \leqslant \sum_{t \in [T]} E[v_i^t \cdot x_i^t - \bar{p}_i^t] + q^T = E[U_i^*] + q^T$$

which leads to Equation (3.9).

On the other hand, since $\mathcal{M}$ satisfies (DIC), we know that $E[U_i^*]$ cannot be more than the utility of truthfully reporting $E[U_i]$, hence

$$E[\tilde{U}_i^*] \leqslant E[U_i^*] + q^T \leqslant E[U_i] + q^T \tag{3.10}$$

We then provide a lower bound on one's expected cumulative utility in $\tilde{\mathcal{M}}$ when reporting truthfully, denoted as $E[\tilde{U}_i]$.

According to the proof of Theorem 3.1, we know that with high probability the credit c_i^t is always close to zero, i.e.,

$$\Pr[\forall t, \ c_i^t + q^t \geqslant 0 \text{ and } c_i^{T+1} \leqslant q^T] \geqslant 1 - \delta$$

In this case, $\forall t \in [T]$, $\alpha_i^t = 1$. Hence buyer i's allocations are identical with that of truthfully reporting under the original mechanism $\mathcal{M}$, i.e., $\tilde{x}_i^{1:T} = x_i^{1:T}$. Again, by Equation (3.5) and Equation (3.6),

$$\sum_{t\in[T]} \tilde{p}_i^t = c_i^{T+1} + \sum_{t\in[T]} \bar{p}_i^t \leqslant q^T + \sum_{t\in[T]} \bar{p}_i^t$$

where the last inequality is implied by $\alpha_i^T = 1$.

Hence, in this case,

$$
\begin{aligned}
\mathrm{E}[\tilde{U}_i] &= \mathrm{E}\left[\sum_{t\in[T]} v_i^t \cdot \tilde{x}_i^t - \tilde{p}_i^t\right] = \mathrm{E}\left[\sum_{t\in[T]} v_i^t \cdot x_i^t - \tilde{p}_i^t\right] \\
&\geqslant \mathrm{E}\left[\sum_{t\in[T]} v_i^t \cdot x_i^t - \bar{p}_i^t\right] - q^T \\
&= \mathrm{E}[U_i] - q^T
\end{aligned}
$$

Otherwise, if there exists $t \in [T]$ such that $\alpha_i^t < 1$ or $c_i^{T+1} > q^T$, ex-post IR implies that buyer i's cumulative utility must always be non-negative.

Combining the cases above, we conclude that

$$\mathrm{E}[\tilde{U}_i] \geqslant (1 - \delta)(\mathrm{E}[U_i] - q^T),$$

$$\mathrm{E}[\tilde{U}_i] \geqslant \mathrm{E}[U_i] - \left(\frac{\delta}{1-\delta}\mathrm{E}[\tilde{U}_i] + (1-\delta)q^T\right)$$

Applying the upper bound Equation (3.10) yields:

$$\mathrm{E}[\tilde{U}_i] \geqslant \mathrm{E}[\tilde{U}_i^*] - \left(\frac{\delta}{1-\delta}\mathrm{E}[\tilde{U}_i] + (2-\delta)q^T\right)$$

By setting $\delta = \dfrac{1}{T+1}$, we have $\dfrac{\delta}{1-\delta} = \dfrac{1}{T}$, and clearly q^T is still in $\tilde{O}(\sqrt{T})$. Since $\mathrm{E}[\tilde{U}_i] \leqslant T\bar{v}$, we get

$$\mathrm{E}[\tilde{U}_i] \geqslant \mathrm{E}[\tilde{U}_i^*] - (2q^T + \bar{v})$$

Therefore, the credit account mechanism $\tilde{\mathcal{M}}$ is approximately truthful with $\epsilon = 2q^T + \bar{v} = \tilde{O}(\sqrt{T})$.

3.1.7 Impossibility Result

As a complement to the constructed ϵ-IC and ex-post IR credit account mechanism, we show that dominant-strategy IC and ex-post IR cannot be achieved simultaneously by any non-trivial mechanisms.

Theorem 3.3 *No non-trivial mechanism achieves both dominant-strategy IC and ex-post IR at the same time.*

Proof To satisfy Equation (DIC), reporting truthfully must be the best action of a buyer for any realization of $F^{1:T}$ and $v^{1:T}$.

Let $\mathcal{M}$ be any ex-post individual rational mechanism. In any period t, suppose i is the winner in period t. For any $t' \in (t, T]$, let $F_i^{t'}$ be the distribution that $v_i^{t'} = 0$ with probability 1, while other buyers have positive expected values.

Therefore, buyer i has no incentive to win after the period t. So buyer i's best action is always to report 0 after getting the item in period t, which results in 0 payment.

Thus, for $\mathcal{M}$ to be dominant-strategy incentive compatible, $\mathcal{M}$ must charge the winner 0 at period t. Otherwise, the above realization of $F_i^{t'}$ becomes a counter-example. Since t is any period, it follows that $\mathcal{M}$ charges the winner 0 in every period. So any mechanism that satisfies the two properties simultaneously must be trivial.

3.2 Dynamic Reserve Pricing via Reinforcement Mechanism Design①

In many social systems in which individuals and organizations interact with each other, there can be no easy laws to govern the rules of the environment, and agents' payoffs are often influenced by other agents' actions. In this section, we examine such a social system: the

① This section was originally published as reference [35]: Weiran Shen, Binghui Peng, Hanpeng Liu, Michael Zhang, Ruohan Qian, Yan Hong, Zhi Guo, Zongyao Ding, Pengjun Lu and Pingzhong Tang. Reinforcement Mechanism Design, with Applications to Dynamic Pricing in Sponsored Search Auctions[C]// Proceedings of the 34th AAAI Conference on Artificial Intelligence, 2018: 2236-2243. Copyright © 2020, Association for the Advancement of ArtificialIntelligence The material has been reproduced here with the permission of the AAAI Press.

sponsored search auctions and tackle the search engine's dynamic pricing problem by applying the AI-driven mechanism design framework. In this setting, the environment not only changes over time, but also behaves strategically. Over repeated interactions with the bidders, the search engine can dynamically change the reserve prices and determine the optimal strategy that maximizes the profit. We first train a buyer behavior model, with a real bidding data set from a major search engine, that predicts bids given information disclosed by the search engine and the bidders' performance data from previous rounds. We then formulate the dynamic pricing problem as an MDP and apply a reinforcement-based algorithm that optimizes reserve prices over time. Experiments demonstrate that our model outperforms static optimization strategies including the ones that are currently in use as well as several other dynamic ones.

3.2.1 Background

Selling advertisements online through sponsored search auctions is a proven profit model for Internet search engine companies such as Google and Baidu. When a user submits a query to such a search engine, it displays, on the result page, a few advertisements alongside the organic results, both related to the query. In the backend, the keyword search triggers an auction mechanism among all advertisers who are interested in the keyword. The advertisers submit bids to compete for advertising positions on the result page. The search engine then ranks the advertisements on the result page according to the advertisers' bids and charges them only when someone clicks on the advertisements.

The gold-standard mechanism in sponsored search is the well-known *generalized second price (GSP) auction*[3, 8]. The auctions allocate the best slots to the advertisers who submit the highest bids, second best slots to the ones with the second highest bids, and so on; and charge them based on the bids one slot below them (or the lowest prices for them to maintain the current slot). Major search engines all adopt some variants of the GSP auction.

A problem with the vanilla GSP auction is that it is not revenue optimal, according to the seminal theory[7, 36]. It is known that, under standard game theory assumptions, a revenue-optimal auction does not necessarily allocate the slots by the rank of their bids. It is also known that in an optimal auction, there exists a vector of advertiser-specific reserve prices that filter low bids. Over the years, a large body of literature at the interface of economics and computer science has focused on revenue optimization of GSP auctions by incorporating insights (ranking and reserve price) from Myerson's theory [37-41].

However, most revenue optimization theories depend crucially on the assumptions about the bidders' rational behaviors. Recently, it has been shown that such assumptions may not hold in reality. Therefore, an emerging line of works has started to focus on settings where the bidders use a certain learning algorithm[34,42-43]. However, most of these models do not give a specific and detailed description of the bidders' actual behaviors. Also, the different rationality levels of the heterogeneous bidder population cannot be easily captured.

3.2.1.1 The AI-Driven Approach

Instead of applying the mechanism design theory or machine learning techniques in isolation, we apply the AI-driven mechanism design framework to examine how a social system with human players can be better designed. First, we follow the mechanism design theory and describe our mechanism with a set of parameters. Then we apply optimization algorithms to search for the optimal parameters. Meanwhile, in order to tackle the so-called "second-order" effect (bidders have different behaviors under different mechanisms), we use machine learning algorithms to build a bidder behavior model that depends on mechanism parameters.

The first part of Section 3.2 tries to solve the problems mentioned above by building an end-to-end neural network-based bidder behavior model. Our model consists of both a public feature set and a private feature set, and directly predicts a bidder's bidding behaviors using the features that are observable by the bidder. Our model scales well with extremely large datasets and can also handle heterogeneous bidders due to the great flexibility of neural networks.

In the second part of Section 3.2, we formulate our bidder behavior model mathematically as a Markov model. And enabled by this, we can view the dynamic mechanism design problem as a Markov decision process (MDP). We then solve the MDP with reinforcement learning techniques. Specifically, our objective is to design a mechanism so the performance of the system can be improved through the change of some policy parameters even in the presence of strategic players in the system. This modification of the setting creates several significant challenges. First, the system is not static anymore. In each round, the algorithm will attempt to change some policy parameters for optimal mechanism design. This changes the environment for the players. Second, at the same time when the rule is changing, the players' strategies change too. They can adopt complex strategies to react to changing rules. This moving-target nature of the setting makes it difficult to optimize the mechanism. Third, as in the traditional setting, reinforcement learning requires a large number of feedback for the training, but tweaking the environment is usually very costly.

This approach is also clearly different from the classic mechanism design theory. We relax some unrealistic assumptions such as quasi-linear utility and bidders' rationality. Instead, we utilize machine learning algorithms to learn bidder behaviors.

We consider the setting of sponsored search auctions and explore the use of an AI-driven mechanism so that search engines can dynamically set minimum allowed bids and use the data generated in the process to maximize the profit. The proposed algorithm can be generalized and applied to other settings to improve system design.

We make the following two major contributions by applying the AI-driven mechanism design framework:

- We propose a neural network-based bidder behavior model. Our model follows the rich research literature on behavioral economics[44-46]. Our choice of RNN is commonly used to deal with time series data. Based on this, we also provide a Markov behavior interpretation, which enables us to use tools from other domains to search for a dynamic mechanism with good enough performance;
- Based on the above bidder behavior model, we model the dynamic mechanism design problem as a Markov decision process, and use the Monte-Carlo tree search algorithm to find a dynamic mechanism that has much better performance than the current

one online.

A version of our framework has already been implemented in the online ad auction system in Baidu, and has been proven to be able to significantly increase the revenue (see Baidu's Financial Report of Q1 2018[1]).

3.2.1.2　Related Works

In the AI community, a recent, interesting line of works aims to tackle the revenue optimization problem from a dynamic learning perspective. Mohri and Medina[47-48] apply learning algorithms to exploit past auctions as well as user features. Their algorithms mainly focus on the estimation of the underlying bid distribution, thus relying on the implicit assumption that buyers do not change their behaviors over time. Mohri and Medina[49-50] aim to optimize revenue with strategic buyers who aim to maximize their cumulative discounted surplus. They give desirable regret bounds to online pricing algorithms. These works assume that there is an underlying value or value distribution for each buyer and it does not change over time.

Battaglini[51] study the Markovian consumer model in a long-term contract setting. Their results show that even when the types at different times are highly persistent, the optimal contract is far from a static one. He et al.[52] and Tian et al.[53] also assume that buyers' behaviors have the Markov property. In particular, Tian et al.[53] focus on buyer behavior predictions and use a truncated Gaussian distribution as the transition probability. Their goal is to find the best static mechanism, and restrict their buyer model to be a linear combination of several simple behavior patterns.

Different from these works, our model allows changes in the underlying value distribution and does not rely on simple assumptions of the bidders' behaviors.

One objective of many existing works in the literature of sponsored search auctions is to improve the revenue of GSP auctions[9, 10, 37, 41]. When designing and analyzing these auctions, most of these works make the standard game-theoretical assumption that advertisers have a single parameter called *type* that indicates their maximum willingness-to-pay for a single click-through. When evaluating these auctions, these works also assume that advertisers are rational and will play according to some equilibrium.

While these works shed light on how to design sponsored search auctions in theory, the assumptions they make do not generally hold in the practice of keyword auctions. For example, most advertisers have complex preferences and private information, such as budget constraints[54-56], multi-dimensional valuations, and negative externalities[57-58]. Furthermore, private information such as budget may change dynamically over time and advertisers may not be able to observe all configuration parameters of the auction.

There are a few exceptions in the literature that take the initiative to design and evaluate sponsored search auctions by getting rid of these assumptions. Ostrovsky and Schwarz[39] conduct large field experiments on manually setting different levels of reserve prices in sponsored search auctions and evaluate these designs. They show, with A/B tests, that by incorporating discounted Myerson's reserve prices, the search engine (Yahoo! in this case) can improve its revenue. However, it remains unclear about the long-term performance of these auctions since all these auctions are assumed to be static. It is also unclear how the *ad hoc* selection of the reserve prices can be improved. Nekipelov et al.[42] investigate the problem of estimating the valuations of the advertisers from their bids in the GSP auction. They get rid of the standard assumption that the bidders must bid according to equilibrium and make a milder assumption that the bidders play according to some no-regret learning strategy. They characterize the set of possible valuations given a set of bids.

Deep reinforcement learning methods have successfully produced AI agents that can beat human players in video games and the game Go[59-60]. A recent paper by DeepMind[61] proposes "imagination-augmented agents" and applies the method to a Sokoban video game in which the player needs to move boxes to given target locations. With a pre-trained model based on simple levels, the AI agent can solve more difficult levels, demonstrating interesting learning capabilities. Beyond games, deep reinforcement learning shows the powerful potential of developing control policies in physical systems. For example, Abbeel et al.[62] use a reinforcement learning method to fly a helicopter and Tai et al.[63] report that models trained in a simulator can be adopted by real robots. In all these settings, the environment is given and the agents' payoffs are easily determined based on the rules of the environment.

3.2.2 Settings and Preliminaries

In this section, we briefly introduce the sponsored search auction setting we study and define a class of parameterized mechanisms that our algorithm will be optimizing.

3.2.2.1 Sponsored Search Auction and Baidu's Design

We consider an auction design problem in the sponsored search setting. When a user types a keyword query in a search engine, the search engine (called the seller hereafter) displays, on the result page, a few advertisements related to the keyword. We consider auctions of a single keyword, where N bidders compete for K slots. The seller allocates the slots by an auction, and each bidder i reports a bid b_i to the seller. A bid profile is denoted by $b = (b_1, b_2, \cdots, b_N)$. We slightly abuse notations and use b_i to refer to both bidder i and his bid.

In a standard game-theoretical model, there is a single-dimensional type for each bidder that denotes the maximum amount of money that the bidder is willing to pay. However, we do not explicitly emphasize such a value in our model. The reason is two-fold: first, our model does not assume that the bidders are fully rational or rational according to some metric. Second, many factors may affect bidders' bidding behaviors, so explicitly defining one such parameter that we cannot observe does not help much in end-to-end training. These are also the reasons why our bidder behavior model is defined over, instead of their private information, the bidders' observations and past bidding data. In fact, this kind of data-driven model is not uncommon in the literature (see references [52, 54, 64] for example).

We attempt to relax the unrealistic assumptions and consider an environment in which bidders can have arbitrarily complex private information and arbitrary rationality levels that can change dynamically over time. Our goal is to design dynamic mechanisms that yield competitive revenue in practice in the long run. While the AI-driven framework and the algorithms proposed in this section apply to search engines in general, we focus on the sponsored search auction design of Baidu, the largest search engine in China. We use Baidu as a running example and calibrate our model with its data.

Baidu sells 3 ad slots for most keywords and like other major search engines, Baidu runs a type of randomized, GSP-like auction mechanism to sell the slots. The bidding data yielded by the randomness of the mechanism provides a perfect setting for us to learn how bidders react to different choices of reserve prices and the number of impressions, and the induced click-through-rates (CTRs).

3.2.2.2   The GSP Mechanism

The GSP (generalized second price) auction is widely adopted by major search engines. Suppose there are N bidders, competing for K advertising slots. The K slots have different effects of attracting user clicks (described by their CTRs). Denote by q_K the CTR of the K-th slot and assume that q_K is non-increasing with respect to the position of the slot, i.e. $q_1 \geqslant q_2 \geqslant \cdots \geqslant q_K \geqslant 0$. Upon receiving a keyword query, the seller first collects the bid profile b from the bidders. Usually, each bidder is associated with a reserve price r_i, which is the minimum bid that bidder i needs to place in order to enter the auction. Denote by $b_{(i)}$ the i-th highest bid among those above the reserve prices. The seller then sequentially allocates the i-th slot to bidder $b_{(i)}$, until either the slots or the bidders run out. When bidder $b_{(i)}$'s advertisement is clicked by a user, the seller charges the bidder according to the following rule:

$$
p_{(i)} = \begin{cases} \max \left\{ \dfrac{q_{i+1} b_{(i+1)}}{q_i}, r_{(i)} \right\}, & b_{(i+1)} \text{ exists} \\ r_{(i)}, & \text{otherwise} \end{cases}
$$

The reserve price profile r can significantly affect the revenue of the platform. We view the reserve price profile r as the main parameters of the mechanism. The seller's goal is to set reserve price profiles dynamically to maximize its revenue.

3.2.3   Bidder Behavior Model

The mechanism design theory relies crucially on how the bidders behave. The classical game theoretical analysis depends on the following assumptions:

- The bidders have quasi-linear utility;
- The bidders have unlimited information access and computational power to compute a Nash equilibrium.

However, these assumptions become problematic in the real world. First, different bidders may have different advertising campaigns with different objectives. For example, a bidder who wants to increase the awareness of his brand may only care about the number of impressions he could obtain, while a bidder with budget constraints who aims to increase the sales volume of his products may focus on the number of clicks of his advertisement in a specific slot. Second, in real advertising platforms, the bidders can only access information about their own advertisements. Empirical evidence has also shown that the above assumptions may not hold in sponsored search auctions[64-65].

3.2.3.1   RNN-Based Bidder Model

In our model, in each time period, a bidder's action is just his bid distribution. The reason why the bid forms a distribution is that a bidder may place different bids for different user characteristics. Each bidder i can be represented by a function g_i that takes as input the history bid distributions and KPIs (key performance indicators) of bidder i, and outputs the bidder's bid distribution of the next time step. To fit these time series data, we implement a standard Long Short-Term Memory (LSTM) recurrent neural network with 128 hidden units via TensorFlow (see Figure 3.1). The output of the RNN is further transformed through a common fully connected layer with a softmax activation function to ensure that the final output of the network is a valid probability distribution. We set the time step to be 1 day. The inputs of the network include KPIs of m consecutive days (a comparison of the performance for different m's can be seen in Figure 3.2), the bid distributions for the bidder, and also some date-related features.

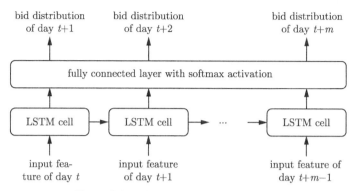

Figure 3.1   RNN bidder behavior model

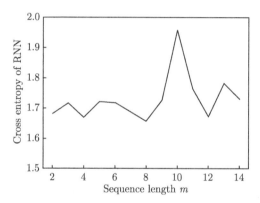

Figure 3.2   Performance of different sequence lengths

Baidu sets both a minimum bid $\underline{b}$ and a maximum bid $\bar{b}$ and allows the bidders to bid any integer value between them (typically $\underline{b} = 10$ and $\bar{b} = 100000$). To simplify the representation, we discretize the bid distribution with 100 non-overlapping intervals and use a 100-dimensional vector b to describe a bid distribution. So $\sum_{j=1}^{100} b_j = 1$ and $\forall 1 \leqslant j \leqslant 100$, $b_j \geqslant 0$ is the probability that the bidder's bid falls in the j-th interval. These 100 intervals are computed according to historical data so that each interval covers roughly the same number of bids placed by all bidders.

Our choice of KPI statistics for each bidder includes the number of impressions the bidder obtains from each slot, the total number of obtained clicks and the total amount of payments. Our observation in Baidu shows that the bidders care more about relative changes in their

KPIs rather than absolute changes. For example, an increase of 100 clicks makes no difference at all for a bidder obtaining 2 million clicks every day, but can be quite significant for a small bidder obtaining 200 daily clicks. Therefore, to capture such relative changes, we use the logarithm values of these KPI statistics as the input features to our RNN and encode them with tile-coding.

Besides the above private features, we also include a public feature set, including date-related features such as the month and the day of the week. All of these features are encoded with one-hot encoding. The reason for including these features is that most advertisers have seasonal advertising campaigns and may adjust their bidding strategies according to the current date.

Table 3.1 gives a list of features used in our bidder model. Similar to text generation tasks, the bid distribution appears in both the input and the output of our network. However, the two distributions are for different days. The bid distribution of day $t + 1$ is computed according to that of previous m days (see Equation (3.11)).

Table 3.1   List of features

Feature	Representation
bid distribution	100-dimensional vector
#impressions from different slots	tile-coding of logarithm value
#clicks	
total payment	
month of campaign season	one-hot encoding
day of month	
day of week	

3.2.3.2   Experiments

We select 400 keywords[①] that meet the following conditions:

- The number of daily queries for the keyword is large and stable (with a small variance);

---

① Our dataset is considerably larger than that in most papers in the literature. For example, Nekipelov et al. [42] conduct experiments based on 1 week's data from 9 bidders and the dataset for simulations in reference [37] contains only 1 keyword.

- The most part (at least 80%) of the revenue of the keyword is contributed by at most 3 bidders.

We extract 8 months' bidding data related to these keywords from Baidu. The total data size of the data set is over 70 TB. As mentioned in Section 3.2.4.1, the reason for the second condition is that the effect of reserve prices diminishes in thick markets. These 400 keywords in the data set contribute about 10% of Baidu's total revenue. In our data set, each data record corresponds to an impression of an ad and contains over 300 data fields. The main fields of a record and their formats are listed in Table 3.2. The CTR values are stored using integer numbers instead of floating numbers for robustness reasons.

Table 3.2 Data fields and their formats

Data field	Format
query id	hash value
keyword id	hash value
bidder id	hash value
user id	hash value
bid (cent)	integer value $\in [10, 100000)$
CTR	integer value $\in [0, 10^6]$, which is the true CTR value multiplied by 10^6
slot number	integer value $\in [1, 3]$
number of clicks	integer value $\in [0, \infty]$
payment (cent)	integer value $\in [0, \infty]$
display time	string, e.g., "2017-03-22 17:24:35"
device type	string, e.g., "iOS"
...	...

For each keyword, we only focus on the 3 major bidders and ignore others. For each bidder, we build an LSTM recurrent neural network and train it using the 8 months' data. We use the average cross entropy as the performance indicator and optimize our RNN using Tensorflow's built-in ADAM optimizer. The total data set is divided into a 90% training set and a 10% test set.

Recall that the input of our RNN is the bid distributions and KPIs of m consecutive days. We train our network for different m's and their performances are shown in Figure 3.2. Both $m = 4$ and $m = 8$ achieve similar performances. We choose the one with a simpler structure (i.e., $m = 4$) which has an average cross-entropy of about 1.67 among all bidders and all test instances in the test set. Some selected test instances are listed in Figure 3.3.

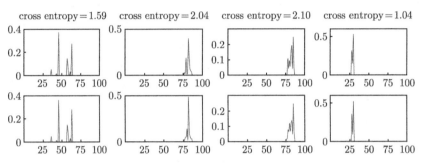

Figure 3.3   Prediction results for 4 selected bidders

Each sub-figure contains two distributions, with the upper one being the actual distribution and the lower one being the prediction. The cross entropy of each sub-figure is shown on top

The prediction of our network is quite accurate according to Figure 3.3. One might argue that the bidders may be very "lazy" and do not often change their bids, and in this case, obtaining an accuracy as shown in Figure 3.3 is not significant at all. However, our previous online experiment shows that the bidders actually change their bids quite frequently. We also simulated this experiment offline using only our bidder model and get very similar results as the online experiment (see Section 3.2.4.3). In fact, the most recent data in our dataset is from the day just before the online experiment was conducted.

3.2.3.3   Markov Formulation

Similar to reference [52] and reference [54], we adopt the time-homogeneous Markov model to interpret the RNN-based bidders' behavior model. Denote by $s_i^{(t)}$ and $h_i^{(t)}$ the bid distribution of bidder i and the KPIs received by bidder i at time step t. The bidders may adjust their bids dynamically according to their KPIs. Thus the bid distribution of bidder i at the next time step is a function of previous s_i's and h_i's:

$$s_i^{(t+1)} = g_i\left(s_i^{(t-m+1:t)}, h_i^{(t-m+1:t)}\right) \tag{3.11}$$

where $s_i^{(t-m+1:t)}$ and $h_i^{(t-m+1:t)}$ are bidder i's bid distributions and KPIs of m consecutive time steps. Note that the above equation models a Markov chain of order m. Similar models are commonly used in the literature, see references [51-52]. Our experiences with Baidu also indicate that the Markov model aligns with the bidders' behaviors.

3.2.4 Dynamic Mechanism Design as Markov Decision Process

In this section, we describe how we formulate the dynamic mechanism design problem as an MDP and how we solve it using reinforcement learning techniques.

When faced with such a problem, one may naïvely think of it as a searching problem and model it with a multi-armed bandit model (say, contextual bandit). However, there are two major challenges with bandit models. Firstly, classic multi-armed-bandit models make the assumption that the reward of pulling each arm is independent of the pulling time and the underlying reward distribution does not change over time. However, in practice we often find that each bidder's behavior is correlated with his historical behaviors, violating the independence assumption. Secondly, in order to apply bandit models to our setting, we have to regard each reserve price profile as an "arm", the number of arms is thus exponential in the number of bidders.

Another closely related solution is deep reinforcement learning. Although our framework is very similar to reinforcement learning, there are also fundamental differences. First, in reinforcement learning, the agent usually interacts with a non-strategic environment, meaning that, although maybe unknown in advance, the state transition function does not change over time. However, in our setting, the bidders are strategic and may change their bidding strategies. This is equivalent to a case in reinforcement learning where the environment changes the transition probabilities to benefit itself. Second, our framework combines machine learning and mechanism design theory. Without the guidance of this theory, it can be extremely difficult to build a model for the environment. And due to the strategic nature of the bidders, it is also very difficult for model-free reinforcement learning algorithms to find the optimal solution. Third, knowledge of economic mechanism design enables us to simplify our model and helps our algorithm to converge quickly, making such a difficult problem tractable.

Enabled by our bidder behavior model, we can formulate the dynamic mechanism design problem as a Markov decision process.

The bids of the N bidders are drawn from their bid distributions. We make the assumption that the individual bids are independent of each other. While such an assumption loses generality, it is actually quite commonly used in the literature[48, 52]. The joint bid distribution is

$$s^{(t+1)} = \prod_{i=1}^{N} s_i^{(t+1)} = \prod_{i=1}^{N} g_i \left(s_i^{(t-m+1:t)}, h_i^{(t-m+1:t)} \right)$$

$$= g \left(s^{(t-m+1:t)}, h^{(t-m+1:t)} \right)$$

For simplicity, we assume that the number of daily queries of each keyword is constant. Thus, the KPI $h^{(t)}$ is completely determined by both the bid distribution $s^{(t)}$ and the reserve price profile $r^{(t)}$.

Thus we can formulate the dynamic mechanism design problem as a Markov decision process, where we view $s^{(t)}$ as the state of the seller and $r^{(t)}$ as its action.

Definition 3.5 The long-term revenue maximization problem is a Markov decision process $(\mathcal{N}, S, R, G, \text{REV}(s, r), \gamma)$, where

- $\mathcal{N}$ is the set of bidders with $|\mathcal{N}| = N$;
- $S = S_1 \times \cdots \times S_N$ is the state space, where S_i is the set of all possible bid distributions of bidder i;
- $R = R_1 \times \cdots \times R_N$ is the action space, where R_i is the set of all possible reserve prices that the mechanism designer can set for bidder i;
- $G = (g_1, g_2, \cdots, g_N)$ is the set of state transition functions;
- $\text{REV}(s, r)$ is the immediate reward function that gives the expected revenue for setting reserve price profile r when the state is s;
- γ is the discount factor with $0 < \gamma < 1$.

Remark 3.1 Note that we can change the immediate reward from the revenue to any other function without changing the framework.

The objective is to select a sequence of reserve price profiles $\{r^{(t)}\}$ that maximizes the sum of discounted revenues:

$$OBJ = \sum_{t=1}^{\infty} \gamma^t \text{REV}\left(s^{(t)}, r^{(t)}\right)$$

Figure 3.4 shows the main framework of the dynamic mechanism design problem. The framework contains two parts:

- The Markov bidder model (the RNNs in our case, as described in Section 3.2.3), which determines how bidders adjust their bids according to the KPI feedback;
- The mechanism, where the bidders interact with the seller's action (reserve prices) and get KPIs as feedback.

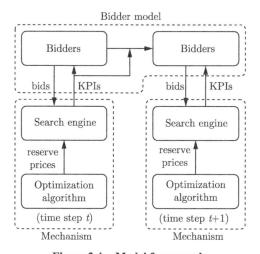

Figure 3.4   Model framework

3.2.4.1   Optimization Algorithm: Monte-Carlo Tree Search

Although an optimal reserve pricing scheme exists according to the MDP theory, its exact computation is formidably costly due to the following reasons:

- The number of possible reserve profiles of our optimization problem grows exponentially with respect to the number of the bidders;
- The number of states to explore is exponential with respect to the search depth.

We circumvent the first difficulty by restricting attention to the keywords that contain only a few major bidders. We focus on the keywords with thin markets (few major bidders) mainly because the effect of reserve prices diminishes in thick markets anyway. To tackle the second one, we only explore possible actions for a bidder to be in a small neighborhood of the current reserve price. This restriction is also necessary for practical stability concerns, since sudden changes in reserve prices would result in sudden changes in bidders' KPIs, which would hurt the stability of the advertising platform. With these restrictions, the size of the action space is greatly reduced to a small subset. To further speed up the search, we implement the *Monte Carlo Tree Search (MCTS) algorithm*[66-67], since the computational complexity of the MCTS algorithm can be effectively bounded by restricting the search depth and the number of search trajectories for each decision.

The MCTS algorithm is an exploration algorithm to evaluate available action values at the current state by running simulations. The MCTS algorithm maintains a tree structure, with its root being the current state. It updates the state values by repeatedly simulating available actions. Though MCTS can be replaced by any other suitable optimization algorithm in our framework, our main reasons to use MCTS are as follows:

- The state space (bid distribution) has uncountably many states, so it is impossible to apply traditional MDP algorithms (value iteration or policy iteration[68]). Even discretization does not help because it still has formidably high dimensions.
- Though deep reinforcement learning grows fast in recent years and succeeds in numerous scenarios, it is inappropriate to train a deep neural network in our setting, i.e. deep Q-learning network (DQN)[59] or asynchronous advantage actor-critic (A3C)[69]. The reason is that a deep neural network depends highly on the bidders' behaviors. Each time we update our bidder behavior model, the entire network needs to be retrained. In addition, we do not have reasonable estimations of the Q-value for each state and action, which will slow down the training process.

Our MCTS algorithm starts with the root node of the search tree, which represents the current state. Before selecting the best reserve price profile, we repeatedly simulate future revenue and bidder responses of choosing each available reserve price profile. In each simulation, the MCTS algorithm chooses a reserve price profile (adds a child node to the search tree) according to some selection rule and estimates the immediate reward as well as the bidders' responses (which is the state of the next time step) using our RNN bidder model. This procedure goes on until the maximum depth of the search tree is reached. Then the algorithm back-propagates the immediate rewards to the root node and updates the corresponding long-term reward. Such a simulation trajectory from the root node to the maximum depth node is also repeated many times to get an accurate estimate of the expected long-term revenue.

In general, our MCTS algorithm contains three separate parts:

(1) Selection. We choose the Upper Confidence Bounds for Trees (UCT) algorithm as our selection strategy[70], which is the famous Upper Confidence Bounds (UCB) algorithm applied to tree search settings. In the UCT, we uniformly select a reserve price profile until each one is selected once. Then the reserve price profile is selected according to:

$$r = \arg\max_{r} \left(node.Q_{s,r} + c_p \sqrt{\frac{\ln(node.n_s)}{node.n_r}} \right)$$

where $node.n_s$ is the number of times we visit $node$, $node.n_r$ is the number of times we select reserve price profile r previously, $node.Q_{s,r}$ is the estimated long term objective (revenue) for choosing reserve price profile r when the current state is s, c_p can be regarded as the parameter to balance exploration and exploitation. The estimated revenue is scaled to the interval $[0,1]$. Although the parameter c_p can be tuned, we set $c_p = \sqrt{2}$ according to the UCB theories[71] for simplicity.

(2) Expansion and Simulation. During the process of exploration, more nodes are added to the tree in the expansion stage. Upon selecting a specific reserve price profile to explore, we simulate the online auctions to derive both the revenue of the platform and all the KPI statistics for each bidder. Then, with these KPI statistics, we are able to compute the bidders' responses for the next time step using our RNN bidder model.

(3) Back-propagation. Various back-propagation strategies have been developed in the reinforcement learning setting[72]. In our back-propagation algorithm, we apply SARSA(λ)[73], which uses λ-return to

update the corresponding state-action value. To be more specific, the long-term revenue is computed as

$$Q_{s_t, r_t} = \sum_{n=1}^{L-1} w_n \text{REV}^{(n)} \left(s^{(t)}, r^{(t)} \right)$$

where L is the maximum depth we explore and $\text{REV}^{(n)} \left(s^{(t)}, r^{(t)} \right)$ is the discounted n-step revenue:

$$\text{REV}^{(n)} \left(s^{(t)}, r^{(t)} \right) = \sum_{i=0}^{n-1} \gamma^i \text{REV} \left(s^{(t+i)}, r^{(t+i)} \right) + \gamma^n \max_r Q_{s_{t+n}, r}$$

and w_n is the corresponding weight satisfying

$$w_n = \begin{cases} (1-\lambda)\lambda^n, & 0 \leqslant n < L-1 \\ \lambda^{L-1}, & n = L-1 \end{cases}$$

The pseudo-code for our back-propagation algorithm is given in Algorithm 1.

ALGORITHM 1: Back-propagation Algorithm for λ-return

   Input: Sample Path: *path*

   $q = 0$

   for $t = L - 1; t > 0; t \leftarrow t - 1$ **do**

       $(node, r, reward) \leftarrow path[t]$

       $node.n_s \leftarrow node.n_s + 1,$

       $node.n_r \leftarrow node.n_r + 1$

       $q \leftarrow q + reward, \delta_Q \leftarrow q - node.Q_{s,r}$

       $node.Q_{s,r} \leftarrow node.Q_{s,r} + (\delta_Q / node.n_r)$

       $q \leftarrow (1 - \lambda) \max_{r^* | node.n_{r^*} \neq 0} [node.Q_{s,r^*}] + \lambda q$

3.2.4.2　Experiments

We explore possible reserve prices for the bidder to be 95%, 100%, and 105% times the current reserve price for the bidder. We set $\lambda = 0.8$ and the search depth to be 5 in our optimization algorithm. In the selection step, we restrict the number of explorations to be 5000. In the expansion step, to estimate the revenue at the selected node, we simulate the auction 5 million times and compute the average revenue as the per-impression revenue of each keyword.

We set the initial reserve price to be $p = \arg\max_b b(1 - F(b))$ where $F(b)$ is the current bid distribution. We call this reserve price static optimal, since this price maximizes the revenue if the bidders do not change their bids. Several algorithms are compared:

- STATIC_OPT: Always use the initial reserve.
- GREEDY: Let the revenue of the current period be REV^t. In each round, we randomly choose a bidder i and change only his reserve price by -5% and simulate auctions for the next period. The revenue is then

$$\text{REV}_i^{t+1} = \text{REV}\left(s^{(t+1)}, \left(0.95r_i^{(t)}, r_{-i}^{(t)}\right)\right)$$

And we choose

$$r^{(t+1)} = \begin{cases} \left(0.95r_i^{(t)}, r_{-i}^{(t)}\right), & \text{REV}_i^{t+1} - \text{REV}^t > 0 \\ \left(1.05r_i^{(t)}, r_{-i}^{(t)}\right), & \text{otherwise} \end{cases}.$$

Notice this method can be seen as a simplified version of the coordinate gradient descend (ascend) method.

- POLICY_GRAD: This algorithm is similar to applying the GREEDY algorithm to each bidder simultaneously, or equivalent to the MCTS policy of looking at only one future time step. In this algorithm, we compute the revenue change for each bidder i and change the reserve price accordingly:

$$r_i^{(t+1)} = \begin{cases} 0.95r_i^{(t)}, & \text{REV}_i^{t+1} - \text{REV}^t > 0 \\ 1.05r_i^{(t)}, & \text{otherwise} \end{cases}.$$

- BAIDU: Current reserve prices used by Baidu.
- STATIC_50: always use 50 cents as the reserve price for all bidders.

Note that Baidu uses randomized reserve prices in its system, while in the above algorithms, all reserve prices are deterministic. The reason for doing so is due to the company's disclosure policy.

We also compare the performance of different frequencies of changing reserve prices by setting the time step Δt in the expansion step of the optimization algorithm[①]. Clearly, changing the reserve prices too frequently can affect the stability of the platform and is not desirable. In this experiment, we only compare the performance of our framework.

3.2.4.3　Results and Analysis

In the first experiment, we change the reserve every day (time step $\Delta t = 1$) in our MCTS algorithm, and compare it with other strategies mentioned above. We simulate 120 days for each strategy. The results of the experiments are shown in Figure 3.5. Revenue is normalized with the converged value of BAIDU. The figure shows that our dynamic strategy outperforms all other strategies.

- The BAIDU curve converges rapidly within just a few days. It goes up slightly at the beginning, mainly because our simulation uses deterministic reserve prices instead of the actual randomized ones;
- The STATIC_OPT curve undergoes a rapid rise on the first day and then followed by a steep fall, which also converges after two weeks.

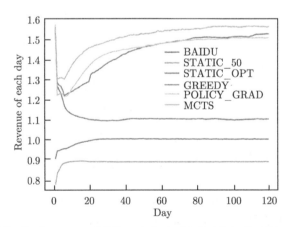

Figure 3.5　Performance of different strategies (see the color figure before)

In fact, in a previous Baidu online experiment, we set STATIC_OPT reserve prices for each (keyword, bidder) pair to test the response from

---

① This time step is not necessarily equal to the time step for training the Markov bidder model. We can always simulate bidder behaviors day by day but change the reserve every several days.

the bidders (see Figure 3.6). The experiment shows that setting a reserve price according to history bids that maximize immediate revenue could result in high revenue in the short term, but drops back after around 10 to 20 days. Furthermore, such a strategy increases the revenue by about 10% after convergence.

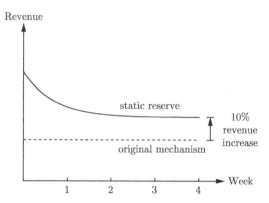

Figure 3.6   Revenue change of a previous online experiment

In our simulations, the STATIC_OPT curve perfectly aligns with observations from the previous online experiment, which can serve as further proof of the accuracy of our bidder behavior model.

Besides, the simulation also reveals some interesting facts about bidder behaviors:

- All aggressive pricing schemes gain high revenue immediately and drop significantly later. This phenomenon is intrinsic for our dataset, since all the bidders undergo a mild pricing mechanism previously due to the moderate choice of reserve prices and the random discounts. The radical changes in reserve prices (from both adopting the static optimal reserve and discarding randomization) could make huge immediate rewards, but once bidders are aware of the change and respond accordingly, less revenue can be extracted.

- Although STATIC_OPT could beat mild mechanisms like BAIDU and STATIC_50, its long-term revenue is not as promising as the short-term. However, by adopting a dynamic mechanism, we can gradually increase daily revenue.

- The experiment shows that with a more involved optimization algorithm (such as MCTS) and an accurate bidder model, we could achieve the best performance and gain higher revenue in the long run.
- Surprisingly, algorithms GREEDY and POLICY_GRAD perform very well, only slightly worse than the MCTS algorithm. However, these two algorithms are much simpler and computationally cheaper. Such a result may, to some extent, suggest that the bidders are not very strategic, since simple algorithms like GREEDY can also capture their behaviors well.
- The GREEDY algorithm and the POLICY_GRAD algorithm are similar to each other, and also have similar performances. The POLICY_GRAD algorithm gives a smoother curve and converges more quickly, but the GREEDY algorithm has a slightly higher revenue when converged.

One may argue that the policies explored in our simulations are too aggressive, and that using personalized reserve prices can cause fairness issues. In fact, the flexibility of our framework allows us to implement other non-aggressive policies, for example, using an anonymous reserve price, or considering other objective functions such as welfare, click yield.

In the second experiment, we compare the effect of the frequency of changing reserve prices. The results are shown in Figure 3.7. We use the

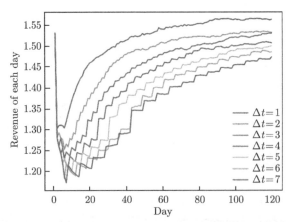

**Figure 3.7　Effect of the frequency of changing reserve prices
(see the color figure before)**

MCTS algorithm and also simulate 120 days for each Δt. Figure 3.7 indicates that the smaller Δt is, the more revenue it can extract, and the more quickly it converges. The revenue of $\Delta t = 7$ is about several percent smaller than that of $\Delta t = 1$. Comparing Figure 3.5 and Figure 3.7, we can see that the performance GREEDY algorithm is almost the same as the MCTS algorithm with $\Delta t = 3$.

References

[1] Baidu Inc. Baidu Inc., first quarter 2018 financial reports [R/OL]. http://ir.baidu.com/static-files/626b8f84-5d34-49b7-b4ab-4f9f03cb8a2b.

[2] SHEN W, WANG Z, ZUO S. Ex-post IR dynamic auctions with cost-per-action payments[C]//Proceedings of the 27th International Joint Conference on Artificial Intelligence. AAAI Press, 2018: 505-511.

[3] EDELMAN B, OSTROVSKY M, SCHWARZ M. Internet advertising and the generalized second-price auction: Selling billions of dollars worth of keywords[J]. The American Economic Review, 97(1): 242-259, 2007.

[4] SPENCER S[EB/OL]. Google deems cost-per-action as the 'holy grail'. CNET News, 2007.

[5] LIU Y, ZHANG J, YU H, et al. Reputation-aware continuous double auction[C]//Proceedings of the 28th AAAI Conference on Artificial Intelligence. AAAI Press, 2014.

[6] HAJAJ C, DICKERSON J P, HASSIDIM A, et al. Strategy-proof and efficient kidney exchange using a credit mechanism[C]//Proceedings of the 29th AAAI Conference on Artificial Intelligence. AAAI Press, 2015: 921-928.

[7] MYERSON R B. Optimal auction design[J]. Mathematics of Operations Research, 1981, 6(1): 58-73.

[8] VARIAN H R. Position auctions[J]. International Journal of Industrial Organization, 25(6): 1163-1178, 2007.

[9] HARTLINE J D, ROUGHGARDEN T. Simple versus optimal mechanisms[C]//Proceedings of the 10th ACM Conference on Electronic Commerce. ACM, 2009: 225-234.

[10] SHEN W, TANG P. Practical versus optimal mechanisms[C]//Proceedings of the 16th Conference on Autonomous Agents and MultiAgent Systems. International Foundation for Autonomous Agents and Multiagent Systems, 2017.

[11] BACHRACH Y, CEPPI S, KASH I A, et al.Optimising trade-offs among stakeholders in ad auctions[C]//Proceedings of the Fifteenth ACM Conference on Economics and Computation. ACM, 2014: 75-92.

[12] CAI Y, DASKALAKIS C,WEINBERG S M. An algorithmic characterization of multi-dimensional mechanisms[C]//Proceedings of the Forty-Fourth annual ACM symposium on Theory of Computing. ACM, 2012: 459-478.

[13] DASKALAKIS C, DECKEBAUM A, TZAMOS C. Mechanism design via optimal transport[C]//Proceedings of the fourteenth ACM Conferenceon Electronic Commerce, ACM, 2013: 269-286.

[14] TANG P, WANG Z. Optimal mechanisms with simple menus[J]. Journal of Mathematical Economics, 2017, 69(Complete): 54-70.

[15] YAO ACC. An n-to-1 bidder reduction for multi-item auctions and its applications[C]//Proceedings of 2015 ACM-SIAM Symposium on Discrete Algorithms. Society for Industrial and Applied Mathematics, 2015: 92-109.

[16] YAO ACC. Dominant-strategy versus bayesian multi-item auctions: Maximum revenue determination and comparison[C]//Proceedings of the 2017 ACM Conference on Economics and Computation. ACM, 2017: 3-20.

[17] AMIN K, ROSTAMIZADEH A, SYED U. Learning prices for repeated auctions with strategic buyers[C]//Proceedings of the 26th International Conference on Neural Information Processing Systems. Curran Associates Inc., 2013: 1169-1177.

[18] AMIN K, ROSTAMIZADEH A, SYED U. Repeated contextual auctions with strategic buyers[C]//Proceedings of the 27th International Conference on Neural Information Processing Systems. MIT Press, 2014: 622-630.

[19] KANORIA Y, ZAZERZADEH H. Dynamic reserve prices for repeated auctions: Learning from bids[C]//International Conference on Web and Internet Economics. Springer, 2014: 232-232.

[20] BALSEIRO S, LIN M, MIRROKNI V, et al. Dynamic revenue sharing[C]// Proceedings of the 31st International Conference on Neural Information Processing Systems. Curran Associates, Inc., 2017: 2678-2686.

[21] EPASTO A, MAHDIAN M,MIRROKNI V, et al. Incentive-aware learning for large markets[C]//Proceedings of the 2018 World Wide Web Conference. International World Wide Web Conferences Steering Committee, 2018: 1369-1378.

[22] TANG P, ZENG Y. The price of prior dependence in auctions[C]//Proceedings of the 2018 ACM Conference on Economics and Computation. ACM, 2018: 485-502.

[23] BERGEMANN D, VäLIMäKI J. Dynamic mechanism design: An introduction. Technical report[J]. Cowles Foundation Discussion Papers, 2017.

[24] KLEMPERER P. Auctions with almost common values: The wallet game and its applications[J]. European Economic Review, 1998, 42(3): 757-769.

[25] BERGEMANN D, MORRIS S. Robust predictions in games with incomplete information[J]. Econometrica, 2013, 81(4): 1251-1308.

[26] ZAZERZADEH H, SABERI A, VOHRA R. Dynamic pay-per-action mechanisms and applications to online advertising[J]. Operations Research, 2013, 61(1): 98-111.

[27] HU Y, SHIN J, TANG Z. Incentive problems in performance based online advertising pricing: cost per click vs. cost per action[J]. Management Science, 2015, 62(7): 2022-2038.

[28] AGARWAL N, ATHEY S, YANG D. Skewed bidding in pay-per-action auctions for online advertising[J]. The American Economic Review, 2019,99(2): 441-447.

[29] MIRROKNI V, LEME R P, TANG P, et al. Dynamic auctions with bank accounts[C]//Proceedings of the 25th International Joint Conference on Artificial Intelligence. AAAI Press, 2016: 387-393.

[30] MIRROKNI V, LEME R P, TANG P, et al. Optimal dynamic mechanisms with ex-post IR via bank accounts[P]. arXiv preprint arXiv:1605.08840,2016.

[31] MIRROKNI V, LEME R P, TANG P, et al. Dynamic mechanism design in the field[C]//Proceedings of the 27th International Conferenceon World Wide Web. International World Wide Web Conferences Steering Committee, 2018.

[32] MIRROKNI V, LEME RP, TANG P, et al. Non clairvoyant dynamic mechanism design[C]//Proceedings of the 2018 ACM Conference on Economics and Computation. ACM, 2018: 169-169.

[33] MAHDIAN M, TOMAK K. Pay-per-action model for online advertising[C]//Proceedings of the 3rd International Conference on Internet and Network Economics. Springer-Verlag, 2007: 549-557.

[34] ZAZERZADEH H, SABERI A, VOHRA R, et al. Where to sell: Simulating auctions from learning algorithms[C]//Proceedings of the 2016 ACM Conference on Economics and Computation. ACM, 2016: 597-598.

[35] SHEN W, PENG B, LIU H, et al. Reinforcement mechanism design, with applications to dynamic pricing in sponsored search auctions[C]//Proceedings of the Thirty-Fourth AAAI Conference on Artificial Intelligence. AAAI Press, 2020.

[36] RILEY J G, SAMUELSON W F. Optimal auctions[J]. The American Economic Review, 1981,71(3): 381-392.

[37] LAHAIE S, OENNOCK D M. Revenue analysis of a family of ranking rules for keyword auctions[C]//Proceedings of the 8th ACM Conference on Electronic Commerce. ACM, 2007: 50-56.

[38] ROBERTS B, GUNAWARDENA D, KASH I A, et al.Ranking and tradeoffs in sponsored search auctions[C]//Proceedings of the Fourteenth ACM Conference on Electronic Commerce. ACM, 2013: 751-766.

[39] OSTROCSKY M, SCHWARZ M. Reserve prices in internet advertising auctions: a field experiment[C]//Proceedings of the 12th ACM Conference on Electronic Commerce. ACM, 2011: 59-60.

[40] MILGROM P. Simplified mechanisms with an application to sponsored-search Auctions[J]. Games and Economic Behavior, 2010, 70(1): 62-70.

[41] THOMPSON D R M, LEYTON-BROWN K. Revenue optimization in the generalized second-price auction[C]//Proceedings of the Fourteenth ACM Conference on Electronic Commerce. ACM, 2013: 837-852.

[42] NEKIPELOV D, SYRGKANIS V, TARDOS E. Econometrics for learning Agents[C]//Proceedings of the Sixteenth ACM Conference on Economics and Computation. ACM, 2015: 1-18.

[43] BALSEIRO S R, GUR Y. Learning in repeated auctions with budgets: Regret minimization and equilibrium[C]//Proceedings of the 2017ACM Conference on Economics and Computation. ACM, 2017: 609.

[44] WRIGHT J R, LEYTON-BROWN K. Predicting human behavior in unrepeated, simultaneous-move games[J].Games and Economic Behavior, 2017, 106: 16-37.

[45] WRIGHT J R, LEYTON-BROWN K. Level-0 meta-models for predicting human behavior in games[C]//Proceedings of the Fifteenth ACM Conference on Economics and Computation. ACM, 2014: 857-874.

[46] HARTFORD J, WRIGHT J R, LEYTON-BROWN K. Deep learning for predicting human strategic behavior[C]//Proceedings of the 30th International Conference on Neural Information Processing Systems. Curran Associates, Inc., 2016: 2432-2440.

[47] MOHRI M, MEDINA A M. Learning algorithms for second price auctions with reserve[J].Journal of Machine Learning Research, 2016, 17(74): 1-25.

[48] MOHRI M, MEDINA A M. Non-parametric revenue optimization for generalized second price auctions[C]//Proceedings of the Thirty-First Conference on Uncertainty in Artificial Intelligence. AUAI Press, 2015: 612-621.

[49] MOHRI M, MEDINA A M. Revenue optimization against strategic buyer[C]//Proceedings of the 28th International Conference on Neural Information Processing Systems. MIT Press, 2015: 2530-2538.

[50] MOHRI M, MEDINA A M. Optimal regret minimization in posted-price auctions with strategic buyers[C]//Proceedings of the 27th International Conference on Neural Information Processing Systems. MIT Press, 2014: 1871-1879.

[51] BATTAGLINI M. Long-term contracting with markovian consumers[J]. The American Economic Review, 2005, 95(3): 637-658.

[52] HE D, CHEN W, WANG L, et al. A game-heoretic machine learning approach for revenue maximization in sponsored search[C]//Proceedings of the Twenty-Third International Joint Conference on Artificial Intelligence.AAAI Press, 2013: 206-212.

[53] TIAN F, LI H, CHEN W, et al. Agent behavior prediction and its generalization analysis[C]//Proceedings of the Twenty-Eighth AAAI Conference on Artificial Intelligence. AAAI Press, 2014: 1300-1306.

[54] XU H, GAO B, YANG D, et al. Predicting advertiser bidding behaviors in sponsored search by rationality modeling[C]//Proceedings of the 22nd International Conference on World Wide Web. ACM, 2013: 1433-1444.

[55] ZHOU Y, CHAKRABARTY D, LUKOSE R. Budget constrained bidding in keyword auctions and online knapsack problems[C]//International Workshop on Internet and Network Economics.Springer, 2008: 566-576.

[56] ABRAMS Z. Revenue maximization when bidders have budgets[C]// Proceedings of the Seventeenth Annual ACM-SIAM Symposium on Discrete Algorithm. Society for Industrial and Applied Mathematics, 2006: 1074-1082.

[57] DENG C, PEKEC S. Money for nothing: exploiting negative externalities[C]//Proceedings of the 12th ACM Conference on Electronic Commerce. ACM, 2011: 361-370.

[58] JEHIEL P, MOLDOVANU B, STACCHETTI E. How (not) to sell nuclear weapons[J]. The American Economic Review, 1996: 814-829.

[59] MNIH V, KAVUKCUOGLU K, SILVER D, et al. Human-level control through deep reinforcement learning[J]. Nature, 2015, 518(7540): 529-533.

[60] SILVER D, HUANG A, MADDISON C J, et al. Mastering the game of go with deep neural networks and tree search[J]. Nature, 2016, 529(7587): 484-489.

[61] RACANIÈRE S, WEBER T, REICHERT D, et al. Imagination-augmented agents for deep reinforcement learning[C]//Proceedings of the 31st International Conference on Neural Information Processing Systems, 2017: 5694-5705.

[62] ABBEEL P, COATES A, QUIGLEY M, et al. An application of reinforcement learning to aerobatic helicopter flight[C]//Proceedings of the 19th International Conference on Neural Information Processing Systems. Curran Associates, Inc., 2006: 1-8.

[63] TAI L, PAOLO G, LIU M. Virtual-to-real deep reinforcement learning: Continuous control of mobile robots for mapless navigation[C]//

International Conference on Intelligent Robots and Systems. IEEE, 2017: 31-36.

[64] PIN F, KEY P. Stochastic variability in sponsored search auctions: observations and models[C]//Proceedings of the 12th ACM Conference on Electronic Commerce. ACM, 2011: 61-70.

[65] EDELMAN B, OSTROVSKY M. Strategic bidder behavior in sponsored search auctions[J]. Decision Support Systems, 2007, 43(1): 192-198.

[66] KHANDLWAL P, LIEBMAN E, NIEKUM S, et al. On the analysis of complex backup strategies in Monte Carlo Tree Search[C]//Proceedings of The 33rd International Conference on Machine Learning, 2016: 1319-1328.

[67] BROWNE C B, POWLEY E, WHITEHOUSE D, et al. A survey of Monte Carlo Tree Search methods[J]. IEEE Transactions on Computational Intelligence and AI in Games, 2012, 4(1): 1-43.

[68] BELLMAN R. Dynamic programming[J]. Science, 1966,153(3731): 34-37.

[69] MNIH V, BADIA A P, MIRZA M, et al. Asynchronous methods for deep reinforcement learning[C]//Proceedings of the 33rd International Conference on Machine Learning, 2016: 1928-1937.

[70] KOCSIS L, SZEPESVÁRI C. Bandit based Monte-Carlo planning[C]// European Conference on Machine Learning. Springer, 2006: 282-293.

[71] AUER P, CESA-BIANCHI N, FISCHER P. Finite-time analysis of the multiarmed bandit problem[J]. Machine Learning, 2022,47(2-3): 235-256.

[72] SUTTON R S, BARTO A G. Reinforcement learning: An introduction, volume 1[M]. MIT Press, 1998.

[73] RUMMERY G A. Problem solving with reinforcement learning[D]. University of Cambridge, 1995.

Chapter 4   Multi-Objective Mechanism Design via AI-Driven Approaches

In Section 1.1, we define both the social welfare and the revenue of a mechanism. Designing revenue-optimal auctions is the most important objective in both mechanism design theory and application. Such a research agenda has been intensively studied during the past few decades. However, in some real-world applications, the mechanism designer may also care about other objectives, such as the social welfare. Unfortunately, in general, no mechanism can optimize these objectives simultaneously. For example, in single-item auctions, the Myerson auction optimizes the revenue, while the second price auction maximizes the social welfare. This initiates a line of works that focuses on how to design mechanisms that can tradeoff between different objectives.

In this chapter, we aim to balance these different objectives using AI approaches. Section 4.1 concentrates on the *single parameter setting*, where each buyer's type can be fully characterized by a single parameter. We propose a class of mechanisms, each specified by a parameter α. We show that both the revenue and the social welfare are monotone with respect to the parameter α, meaning that the seller can easily tradeoff between the revenue and the social welfare through simple parameter tuning. Furthermore, we show that any mechanism in our mechanism class can guarantee an approximation ratio of the optimal. This ratio depends on the parameter α and is always better than 2. Therefore, while tuning the parameter α, the seller does not need to worry about significant revenue losses.

Section 4.2 aims to predict good reserve prices for online ad auctions, to tradeoff between the revenue and the *match rate* (the overall probability of a sale) or the welfare. We use a machine learning model that takes as input the context information from the auction and gives a reserve price as output. Starting from the analyses of the market clearing problem, we come up with a loss function that is convex and easy to interpret. Our theoretical analyses show that the match rate is guaranteed to be at least $1 - e^{-1}$. And our experiments show that our method Pareto-dominates (better in every aspect) previous approaches in terms of revenue and match rate.

4.1 Balancing Objectives through Approximation Analysis[①]

Designing simple mechanisms with desirable revenue guarantees has become a major research agenda in the economics and computation community. However, few mechanisms have been actually applied in industry.

In this section, we aim to bridge the gap between the "simple versus optimal" theory and practice, and propose a class of parameterized mechanisms, tailored for the sponsored search auction settings. Our mechanisms can balance different objectives by simple parameter tuning, yet at the same time guarantee near-optimal revenue in both theoretical and practical senses.

4.1.1 Background

Designing revenue-optimal auctions has been one of the most important themes in economics, ever since Myerson's seminal work[2]. Theories for designing such auctions for the so-called "single parameter" environment have been well-developed[3-4], and much progress has been made when selling multiple items[5-7]. Recently, due to the interdisciplinary research paradigm such as algorithmic mechanism design[8] and automated mechanism design [9], and its various applications in the sponsored

① This section was originally published as reference [1]: Weiran Shen, Pingzhong Tang. Practical versus Optimal Mechanisms[C]//Proceedings of the 16th International Conference on Autonomous Agents and MultiAgent Systems, 2017: 78-86.

search auctions[10-11] and other similar domains, it has also become a topic of intensive research at the interface between computer science and economics[12-14].

Following the vein of algorithmic mechanism design, an important literature, initiated by Hartline and Roughgarden[15], aims to design mechanisms that are simple in their forms (e.g., second-price auction with a reserve price) and yet guarantee desirable revenue bounds in the worst case. This viewpoint has turned out to be widely adopted in the economics and computation community and has been investigated under a number of extended domains[8, 16-23].

While a major motivation to design these simple and approximately optimal mechanisms is for the purpose of practicality, unfortunately, to the best of our knowledge, very few of them are actually fielded in industry. From an industrial perspective, there are at least three concerns when considering implementing these mechanisms: first of all, all these mechanisms are designed to guarantee the worst-case revenue bounds, while in industry, the evaluation metric tends to be the average-case performance. Secondly, even though most of these papers are able to guarantee constant approximations, say a 2-approximation, of the optimal revenue, they are still not strong enough in the sense that it may indicate that the seller can lose half of the revenue in certain cases. Last but not least, the seller may have other objectives in addition to the revenue, which are not guaranteed by these mechanisms. These objectives may change dynamically due to various short-term targets of the company.

In this section, we aim to bridge the gap between the "simple versus optimal" theory and practice. To address the concerns raised above, we propose the following refined research agenda, targeting specifically the domain of sponsored search auction design: to design a *parameterized* class of auctions, which

(1) has highly desirable worst-case guarantees (say, better than 2-approximation) of the revenue;

(2) gives flexibility to the engineers, so that they can freely trade off the revenue for other objectives by simply *tuning parameters*;

(3) meets industry-level targets via empirical evaluations.

We investigate the sponsored search auction setting, where the seller has several slots for sale and each slot has a *click-through-rate* (CTR). For ease of presentation, a simpler "K identical items" setting is also considered, which is essentially equivalent to the sponsored search setting with the CTR for each slot being 1. In fact, both the two settings belong to the so-called "single-parameter" setting.

4.1.1.1　Main Contributions

With the above agenda in mind, we make the following contributions, for the sponsored search domain:

- We put forward a parameterized class of auctions, which in essence, rank each bidder by a combined (not necessarily linear) function, described by a single parameter α, of its value and Myerson virtual value, allocate the items (CTRs) greedily according to the rank and charge each bidder according to the so-called *payment identity*.
- We prove that any auction in the parameterized class is a $(2-\theta)$-approximation of the optimal revenue, where θ is between 0 and 1, as a function of the auction parameter α. Furthermore, given any desired θ between 0 and 1, we give explicitly a mechanism that guarantees a $(2-\theta)$-approximation of the optimal revenue.
- We prove that, as the weight of the virtual value increases in the ranking rule, the revenue increases and the welfare drops.
- We empirically evaluate the revenue and the welfare of each auction in this class by simply tuning the parameter α, based on real bidding data.

4.1.1.2　Additional Related Works

The idea of parameterized auctions has been considered by several existing works in the domain of sponsored search auctions. Lahaie and Pennock[24] consider a class of "squashing" mechanisms. They introduce a parameter α and rank the bidders by $b_i w_i^{\alpha}$ where w_i is the CTR of bidder i. They find that setting $\alpha < 1$ generally increases the revenue.

Roberts et al.[25] consider the "anchoring" mechanism that ranks the bidders by $(b_i - r)w_i$. They introduce a reserve price parameter r and a reserve score parameter s. Several ranking algorithms, including $b_i w_i / r$,

$b_i w_i / s$, $b_i w_i^\alpha / s$ and the "squashing" $b_i w_i^\alpha$ are compared. They show, by simulation, that their "anchoring" mechanism achieves more revenue and welfare than other mechanisms.

Bachrach et al.[26] aim towards tradeoffs among different objectives. They use "γ_1 revenue + γ_2 welfare + γ_3 click yield" as their objective function. They show that under the condition $\gamma_1 + \gamma_2 + \gamma_3 = 1$, their mechanism achieves a γ_1 fraction of the optimal revenue, a γ_2 fraction of the optimal welfare and a γ_3 fraction of the optimal click yield. Their work is similar to ours in the sense that they also consider tradeoffs between welfare and revenue. In fact, our class of mechanisms includes their mechanism as a special case (up to a constant factor, which does not affect the outcome of the mechanism) by setting $\alpha = \gamma_1/(\gamma_1 + \gamma_2)$ and $P(t) = Q(t) = t + \gamma_3/(\gamma_1 + \gamma_2)$ ($P(\cdot)$ and $Q(\cdot)$ will be defined later). However, the difference is also very clear: while their goal is to optimize linearly combined objectives and achieve a fraction of the optimal value of these objectives, our goal is to design a class of parameterized mechanisms that are easy for practical use. Also, our mechanisms do not require linear combinations and always achieve an approximation ratio better than 2, which is much stronger than theirs. In addition, our results and their results do not imply each other.

In the same spirit, Procaccia et al.[27] also aim to design a class of parameterized mechanisms, where one can tune the worst-case bound by tuning parameters in the facility location domain.

4.1.2   Settings and Preliminaries

We consider the standard *sponsored search setting*, where N bidders compete for several slots, and each bidder aims at one slot. Each bidder i has a private *valuation* $v_i \geqslant 0$, which is drawn from a publicly known distribution F_i. A *valuation profile* is denoted by $v = (v_1, v_2, \cdots, v_N)$.

Let $\mathcal{X}$ be the set of all feasible allocations. A bidder is said to have *unit-demand* if each element of $x(v)$ is binary. Further, when the bidders have unit-demand, $\mathcal{X}$ has a set representation $\mathcal{X} = \{X(x) \mid x \text{ is feasible}\}$, where $X(x) = \{i \mid x_i = 1\}$. $\mathcal{X}$ is said to be *downward-closed*, if each subset Y of $X \in \mathcal{X}$ is again a feasible allocation.

We focus on both the revenue and the social welfare defined in

Section 1.1. Social welfare is an important metric in practical sponsored search auction design. From the experiences of several major sponsored search teams in China, it is understood that, the number of complaints from advertisers concerning their rankings negatively correlates with the social welfare.

4.1.3　Generalized Virtual-Efficient Mechanisms

In this section, we aim for a tradeoff between the revenue and the social welfare. Our goal is to provide a spectrum of mechanisms, within which one can easily trade off the two objectives. We propose a class of mechanisms, which we call the *generalized virtual-efficient mechanisms*. The meaning of the name will become clear immediately after its formal definition.

Let $P(\cdot)$ and $Q(\cdot)$ be two increasing functions, and assume that each bidder's value distribution satisfies the standard regularity condition[2] (the virtual value function $\varphi(v)$ is increasing with respect to v). We now consider a family of parameterized mechanisms $\mathcal{M}(\alpha, r)$ based on the functions $P(\cdot)$ and $Q(\cdot)$, where α is a real number with $0 \leqslant \alpha \leqslant 1$ and r is a reserve price profile. The mechanism $\mathcal{M}(\alpha, r)$ first filters the bidders with the reserve profile r, then ranks the bidders with the function $\alpha P(v) + (1 - \alpha)Q(\varphi(v))$ among those who meet the reserve price conditions, if any. Finally, the mechanism allocates the items to the agents greedily according to their rankings. Note that $\mathcal{M}(1, r)$ is just the VCG mechanism with reserve profile r, and if $\varphi_i(r_i) = 0$, then $\mathcal{M}(0, r)$ is the optimal auction (denoted by OPT).

4.1.3.1　The K Identical Items Setting

In this section, we consider the setting where the seller has K identical items for sale and each bidder only wants exactly one item (unit demand). This setting is in fact a special case of the sponsored search setting, with all slots' CTRs being 1. We show that in this setting, both the welfare and the revenue change monotonically with respect to the parameter α. In addition, we also provide a tight lower bound for the revenue of our mechanisms.

Theorem 4.1　*Let $P(\cdot)$ and $Q(\cdot)$ be two increasing functions. Suppose that the seller has K identical items for sale and the bidders* *have unit demand. Assume that the distributions F_i that each bidder's valuation is drawn from satisfies the regularity condition. Then* REV $(\mathcal{M}(\alpha, r))$ *is monotone decreasing in α while* WEL$(\mathcal{M}(\alpha, r))$ *is monotone increasing in α.*

Proof For any $0 \leqslant \alpha_1 < \alpha_2 \leqslant 1$, let W_1 and W_2 be the set of winners (those with $x_i = 1$) of $\mathcal{M}(\alpha_1, r)$ and $\mathcal{M}(\alpha_2, r)$, respectively. If the number of bidders who meet the reserve conditions is smaller than or equal to K, then we have $W_1 = W_2$, which contains exactly those who meet the reserve conditions. When the number of bidders who meet the reserve conditions is greater than K, we only need to consider the case where $W_1 \neq W_2$. In this case, both W_1 and W_2 have K winners. It follows that $|W_1 \setminus W_2| = |W_2 \setminus W_1|$.

Since $|W_1 \setminus W_2| = |W_2 \setminus W_1|$, there exist bijections between the two sets. Let μ be any such bijection. For any $i \in W_1 \setminus W_2$, let $j = \mu(i) \in W_2 \setminus W_1$. Since $\mathcal{M}(\alpha_1, r)$ ranks the bidders by $\alpha_1 P(v) + (1 - \alpha_1)Q(\varphi(v))$ and bidder $j \notin W_1$, we have that bidder i has a higher ranking score than bidder j in mechanism $\mathcal{M}(\alpha_1, r)$:

$$\alpha_1 P(v_i) + (1 - \alpha_1)Q(\varphi_i(v_i)) \geqslant \alpha_1 P(v_j) + (1 - \alpha_1)Q(\varphi_j(v_j)) \qquad (4.1)$$

Similarly, mechanism $\mathcal{M}(\alpha_2, r)$ ranks the bidders by $\alpha_2 P(v) + (1 - \alpha_2)Q(\varphi(v))$, and $i \notin W_2$. It follows that:

$$\alpha_2 P(v_j) + (1 - \alpha_2)Q(\varphi_j(v_j)) \geqslant \alpha_2 P(v_i) + (1 - \alpha_2)Q(\varphi_i(v_i)) \qquad (4.2)$$

Multiplying inequality (4.1) by α_2, inequality (4.2) by α_1 and then adding them together yields:

$$\alpha_1\alpha_2 P(v_i) + (1 - \alpha_1)\alpha_2 Q(\varphi_i(v_i)) + \alpha_1\alpha_2 P(v_j) + \alpha_1(1 - \alpha_2)Q(\varphi_j(v_j))$$

$$\geqslant \alpha_1\alpha_2 P(v_j) + (1 - \alpha_1)\alpha_2 Q(\varphi_j(v_j)) + \alpha_1\alpha_2 P(v_i) + \alpha_1(1 - \alpha_2)Q(\varphi_i(v_i))$$

With a little rearrangement, we get

$$(\alpha_2 - \alpha_1)Q(\varphi_i(v_i)) \geqslant (\alpha_2 - \alpha_1)Q(\varphi_j(v_j))$$

Therefore, $Q(\varphi_i(v_i)) \geqslant Q(\varphi_j(v_j))$ since $\alpha_2 - \alpha_1 > 0$. It follows that $\varphi_i(v_i) \geqslant \varphi_j(v_j)$ for $Q(\cdot)$ is an increasing function. Note that the above inequality holds for any $i \in W_1 \setminus W_2$. Summing over all such i, we have

$$\sum_{i \in W_1 \setminus W_2} \varphi_i(v_i) \geqslant \sum_{i \in W_1 \setminus W_2} \varphi_{\mu(i)}(v_{\mu(i)}) = \sum_{i \in W_2 \setminus W_1} \varphi_i(v_i)$$

Thus

$$\begin{aligned} \sum_{i \in W_1} \varphi_i(v_i) &= \sum_{i \in W_1 \cap W_2} \varphi_i(v_i) + \sum_{i \in W_1 \setminus W_2} \varphi_i(v_i) \\ &\geqslant \sum_{i \in W_1 \cap W_2} \varphi_i(v_i) + \sum_{i \in W_2 \setminus W_1} \varphi_i(v_i) \\ &= \sum_{i \in W_2} \varphi_i(v_i) \end{aligned}$$

Taking expectation over v yields:

$$\mathrm{E}_{v \sim F(v)} \left[\sum_{i \in W_1} \varphi_i(v_i) \right] \geqslant \mathrm{E}_{v \sim F(v)} \left[\sum_{i \in W_2} \varphi_i(v_i) \right]$$

which is equivalent to $\mathrm{REV}(\mathcal{M}(\alpha_1, r)) \geqslant \mathrm{REV}(\mathcal{M}(\alpha_2, r))$ by Myerson's Lemma (Lemma 1.1).

Similarly, we can multiply inequality (4.1) by $1 - \alpha_2$ and inequality (4.2) by $1 - \alpha_1$. Adding them together yields:

$$(\alpha_1 - \alpha_2) P(v_i) \geqslant (\alpha_1 - \alpha_2) P(v_j)$$

Thus $P(v_i) \leqslant P(v_j)$ since $\alpha_2 - \alpha_1 > 0$, which implies $v_i \leqslant v_j$. Similarly,

$$\sum_{i \in W_1} v_i \leqslant \sum_{i \in W_2} v_i$$

Taking expectation over v, we have

$$\mathrm{WEL}(\mathcal{M}(\alpha_1, r)) \leqslant \mathrm{WEL}(\mathcal{M}(\alpha_2, r))$$

which completes the proof.

Next, we show that if each distribution F_i satisfies the *monotone hazard rate* (MHR) condition, with appropriate choices of the functions $P(\cdot)$ and $Q(\cdot)$, our mechanisms can achieve approximately optimal revenue.

Definition 4.1 (Hazard Rate) Given a probability distribution $F(v)$, the hazard rate with respect to $F(v)$ is defined to be:

$$h(v) = \frac{f(v)}{1 - F(v)}$$

where $f(v)$ is the density function of the distribution $F(v)$.

If the hazard rate $h(v)$ is monotone increasing with respect to v, we say that the corresponding distribution $F(v)$ satisfies the *monotone hazard rate* condition.

Note that the regularity condition will be automatically satisfied if the hazard rate function is monotone increasing. We first prove a lemma that will be useful later.

Lemma 4.1 *Assume v is distributed according to $F(v)$. Let $\varphi(v)$ and $h(v)$ be the corresponding virtual valuation function and hazard rate function, respectively. Let $P(\cdot)$ and $Q(\cdot)$ be two functions that are increasing, concave and differentiable. Assume there exists a constant $c > 0$, such that the derivatives of $P(\cdot)$ and $Q(\cdot)$ satisfy $\forall v, Q'(v) \geqslant cP'(v) > 0$. Then for all $v > 0$ and all $0 \leqslant \alpha \leqslant 1$,*

$$\alpha P(v) + (1 - \alpha)Q(\varphi(v)) \leqslant R\left(v - \frac{\theta}{h(v)}\right)$$

where $R(v) = \alpha P(v) + (1 - \alpha)Q(v)$ and $\theta = \dfrac{(1 - \alpha)c}{\alpha + (1 - \alpha)c}$.

Proof Let $z = v - \dfrac{\theta}{h(v)}$. Then

$$v = z + \frac{\theta}{h(v)}, \quad \varphi(v) = v - \frac{1 - F(v)}{f(v)} = v - \frac{1}{h(v)} = z - \frac{1 - \theta}{h(v)}$$

Since $P(\cdot)$ and $Q(\cdot)$ are concave functions, we have

$$P(v) \leqslant P(z) + \frac{\theta}{h(v)}P'(z), \quad Q(\varphi(v)) \leqslant Q(z) - \frac{1 - \theta}{h(v)}Q'(z)$$

Thus

$$\alpha P(v) + (1 - \alpha)Q(\varphi(v)) \leqslant \alpha P(z) + (1 - \alpha)Q(z) +$$

$$\frac{\alpha\theta}{h(v)}P'(z) - \frac{(1-\theta)(1-\alpha)}{h(v)}Q'(z)$$

Since $Q'(z) \geqslant cP'(z)$ and $0 \leqslant \alpha \leqslant 1$, $0 \leqslant \theta \leqslant 1$, $h(x) = \dfrac{f(x)}{1-F(x)} > 0$, we have

$$\frac{\alpha\theta}{h(v)}P'(z) - \frac{(1-\theta)(1-\alpha)}{h(v)}Q'(z) \leqslant \frac{\alpha\theta}{h(v)}P'(z) - \frac{(1-\theta)(1-\alpha)}{h(v)}cP'(z)$$
$$= \frac{P'(z)}{h(v)}\left(\alpha\theta - (1-\theta)(1-\alpha)c\right)$$
$$= 0$$

The last equality holds because $\theta = \dfrac{(1-\alpha)c}{\alpha+(1-\alpha)c}$. Therefore

$$\alpha P(v) + (1-\alpha)Q(\varphi(v)) \leqslant \alpha P(z) + (1-\alpha)Q(z) = R(z),$$

which completes the proof.

Next, we show that under certain technical conditions, our mechanism can achieve near-optimal revenue guarantees with appropriate choices of $P(\cdot)$ and $Q(\cdot)$.

Theorem 4.2 *Suppose the distribution F_i satisfies the monotone hazard rate condition, for all i. Let $P(\cdot)$ and $Q(\cdot)$ be two functions that are increasing, concave and differentiable. Assume there exists a constant $c > 0$, such that $\forall v, Q'(v) \geqslant cP'(v) > 0$. Let r^* be the Myerson reserve price profile for the bidders, i.e. $\varphi_i(r_i^*) = 0$. If either one of the following two conditions is satisfied:*

(1) There are K identical items for sale, and the bidders have unit demand;

(2) $P(t) = at$ and $Q(t) = bt$, where a, b are positive constants.

Then $\mathrm{REV}(\mathcal{M}(\alpha, r^*))$ is a $(2-\theta)$-approximation of the optimal mechanism, where $\theta = \dfrac{(1-\alpha)c}{\alpha+(1-\alpha)c}$.

Remark 4.1   These approximation ratios are highly desirable. First, since $\theta \geqslant 0$, all of the approximation ratios are less than 2 (except when $\theta = 0$), which guarantees the near-optimality of our mechanism. Second, the approximation ratio depends on α, which provides more flexibility for practical use. Note that the 2-approximation result by Hartline and Roughgarden[15] is immediate by our result, by setting $P(t) = Q(t) = t$ and $\alpha = 1$.

Proof   Since $\varphi_i(r_i^*) = 0$, we have $r_i^* = \dfrac{1}{h(r_i^*)}$. The MHR condition implies:

$$\frac{1}{h(r_i^*)} \geqslant \frac{1}{h(v_i)}, \forall v_i > r_i^*$$

Thus $\forall v_i > r_i^*$, we have

$$\varphi_i(v_i) + (1-\theta)r_i^* = \varphi_i(v_i) + \frac{1-\theta}{h(r_i^*)} \geqslant \varphi_i(v_i) + \frac{1-\theta}{h(v_i)} = v_i - \frac{\theta}{h(v_i)}$$

It is straightforward that $R(\cdot)$ is an increasing function. Thus $R^{-1}(\cdot)$ exists and is also increasing. So

$$\varphi_i(v_i) + (1-\theta)r_i^* \geqslant v_i - \frac{\theta}{h(v_i)}$$

$$= R^{-1}\left(R\left(v_i - \frac{\theta}{h(v_i)}\right)\right)$$

$$\geqslant R^{-1}\left(\alpha P(v_i) + (1-\alpha)Q(\varphi_i(v_i))\right) \qquad (4.3)$$

The last inequality holds because of Lemma 4.1.

Under condition 1, we always allocate the items to the bidders with the highest ranking scores among those who meet the reserve price condition. Let W and W_{OPT} be the set of winners of our mechanism and the optimal mechanism. Then using similar arguments as in the proof of Theorem 4.1, we have that $|W| = |W_{OPT}|$ and that for any $i \in W \backslash W_{OPT}$ and any $j \in W_{OPT} \backslash W$:

$$\alpha P(v_i) + (1-\alpha)Q(\varphi_i(v_i)) \geqslant \alpha P(v_j) + (1-\alpha)Q(\varphi_j(v_j))$$

which implies:

$$R^{-1}(\alpha P(v_i) + (1-\alpha)Q(\varphi_i(v_i))) \geqslant R^{-1}(\alpha P(v_j) + (1-\alpha)Q(\varphi_j(v_j)))$$

since $R^{-1}(\cdot)$ is increasing.

Under condition 2, we have

$$R(x) = \alpha a x + (1 - \alpha)bx, \quad R^{-1}(x) = \frac{x}{\alpha a + (1 - \alpha)b}.$$

Our mechanism ranks the bidders by $\alpha a v + (1 - \alpha)b\varphi(v)$. Thus

$$\sum_{i=1}^{N} (\alpha a v_i + (1 - \alpha)b\varphi_i(v_i))\, x_i(v) \geqslant \sum_{i=1}^{N} (\alpha a v_i + (1 - \alpha)b\varphi_i(v_i))\, x_i^*(v)$$

where $x(v)$ and $x^*(v)$ is the allocation function of our mechanism and the optimal mechanism, respectively. Equivalently,

$$\sum_{i=1}^{N} \frac{1}{\alpha a + (1 - \alpha)b} (\alpha a v_i + (1 - \alpha)b\varphi_i(v_i))\, x_i(v)$$

$$\geqslant \sum_{i=1}^{N} \frac{1}{\alpha a + (1 - \alpha)b} (\alpha a v_i + (1 - \alpha)b\varphi_i(v_i))\, x_i^*(v)$$

Therefore under both cases, we have

$$\sum_{i=1}^{N} R^{-1}\left(\alpha P(v_i) + (1 - \alpha)Q(\varphi_i(v_i))\right) x_i(v)$$

$$\geqslant \sum_{i=1}^{N} R^{-1}\left(\alpha P(v_i) + (1 - \alpha)Q(\varphi_i(v_i))\right) x_i^*(v) \tag{4.4}$$

According to Myerson's Lemma, the revenue of our mechanism can be written as the weighted expectation of the virtual valuations:

$$\text{REV}(\mathcal{M}(\alpha, r^*)) = \mathbb{E}_{v \sim F(v)}\left[\sum_{i=1}^{N} \varphi_i(v_i) x_i(v)\right] \tag{4.5}$$

The revenue can also be bounded below by r^* since the reserve profile is r^*.

$$\text{REV}(\mathcal{M}(\alpha, r^*)) \geqslant \mathbb{E}_{v \sim F(v)}\left[\sum_{i=1}^{N} r_i^* x_i(v)\right] \tag{4.6}$$

Therefore,

$$(2 - \theta)\text{REV}(\mathcal{M}(\alpha, r^*))$$

$$= \mathbb{E}_{v \sim F(v)} \left[\sum_{i=1}^{N} (\varphi_i(v_i) + (1 - \theta)\varphi_i(v_i)) x_i(v) \right]$$

$$\geqslant \mathbb{E}_{v \sim F(v)} \left[\sum_{i=1}^{N} (\varphi_i(v_i) + (1 - \theta)r_i^*) x_i(v) \right]$$

$$\geqslant \mathbb{E}_{v \sim F(v)} \left[\sum_{i=1}^{N} R^{-1} \left(\alpha P(v_i) + (1 - \alpha)Q(\varphi_i(v_i)) \right) x_i(v) \right]$$

$$\geqslant \mathbb{E}_{v \sim F(v)} \left[\sum_{i=1}^{N} R^{-1} \left(\alpha P(v_i) + (1 - \alpha)Q(\varphi_i(v_i)) \right) x_i^*(v) \right]$$

$$\geqslant \mathbb{E}_{v \sim F(v)} \left[\sum_{i=1}^{N} R^{-1} \left(\alpha P(\varphi_i(v_i)) + (1 - \alpha)Q(\varphi_i(v_i)) \right) x_i^*(v) \right]$$

$$= \mathbb{E}_{v \sim F(v)} \left[\sum_{i=1}^{N} \varphi_i(v_i) x_i^*(v) \right]$$

$$= \text{REV}(OPT)$$

The first inequality combines Equation (4.5) and Equation (4.6). The second inequality comes from Inequality (4.3). The third inequality holds because of Inequality (4.4). The fourth inequality comes from the definition of $\varphi(v)$ and the monotonicity of the functions $P(\cdot)$ and $R^{-1}(\cdot)$. And the last equation is a direct application of Myerson's Lemma.

The first condition can actually be extended to the sponsored search environment (see the Section 4.1.3.2).

Under the second condition, if the set of feasible allocations $\mathcal{X}$ is downward-closed, our bound for the revenue is actually tight. Consider the following example.

Example 4.1   Let $P(t) = Q(t) = t$ and $c = 1$. Suppose there are K items for sale and two groups of bidders EXP and UNI, each containing K bidders, and the bidders inside each group have i.i.d. value distributions. Bidders of EXP have an exponential distribution with $F_{EXP}(v) = 1 - e^{-v}$, while bidders of UNI have values that are distributed uniformly in the interval $\left[\dfrac{1+\alpha-\varepsilon}{e} - \delta, \dfrac{1+\alpha-\varepsilon}{e} + \delta\right]$, where δ, ε are sufficiently small positive numbers. The feasible allocations are those that contain only bidders from the same group. In this case, $\theta = 1 - \alpha$ and our theorem gives an approximation ratio of $1 + \alpha$.

The Myerson reserve prices for bidders in the EXP group and the UNI group are 1 and $\dfrac{1+\alpha-\varepsilon}{e} - \delta$, respectively. For bidders in EXP, the virtual value $\varphi_{EXP}(v) = v - 1$. While the bidders in UNI have virtual value $\varphi_{UNI}(v) = v - 2\delta(1 - F_{UNI}(v))$, which is highly concentrated at a small neighborhood of $\dfrac{1+\alpha-\varepsilon}{e}$. Our mechanism uses a ranking score of $v - 1 + \alpha$ and $v - (1-\alpha)2\delta(1 - F_{UNI}(v))$ for the bidders in EXP and UNI. Again, the ranking score of bidders in UNI is highly concentrated around $\dfrac{1+\alpha-\varepsilon}{e}$. When K is sufficiently large, the number of bidders in EXP that exceeds the reserve price is about $\dfrac{K}{e}$ and the average value of these bidders is about 2. Thus, both the revenue and the total ranking score of allocating to the group UNI are about $\dfrac{(1+\alpha-\varepsilon)K}{e}$, while allocating to the group EXP extracts a revenue of only $\dfrac{K}{e}$ but a total ranking score of $\dfrac{(1+\alpha)K}{e}$. Thus our mechanism allocates the items to EXP, but the optimal mechanism allocates to UNI. The revenue ratio is $1+\alpha-\varepsilon$, which can be arbitrarily close to $1 + \alpha$.

Note that in Theorem 4.2, θ always lies in $[0, 1]$ and changes continuously with respect to α. Thus we can achieve any desired approximation ratio in $[1, 2]$ by simply tuning the α, even if the functions $P(\cdot)$ and $Q(\cdot)$ (and thus the constant c) are fixed, which leads to the following immediate corollary:

Corollary 4.1 *Suppose the distribution F_i satisfies the monotone hazard rate condition for each i. Let $P(\cdot)$ and $Q(\cdot)$ be two functions that are increasing, concave and differentiable. Assume that there exists a constant $c > 0$, such that $\forall v, Q'(v) \geqslant cP'(v) > 0$. Let r^* be the Myerson* *reserve price profile for the bidders, i.e., $\varphi_i(r_i^*) = 0$. If either one of the following two conditions is satisfied:*

(1) There are K identical items for sale, and the bidders have unit-demand;

(2) $P(t) = at$ and $Q(t) = bt$, where a, b are positive constants.

Then for any $\theta \in [0, 1]$, there exists $\alpha \in [0, 1]$, such that the revenue of the mechanism $\mathcal{M}(\alpha, r^*)$ is a $(2 - \theta)$-approximation of that of the optimal mechanism.

4.1.3.2   The Sponsored Search Setting

Now we generalize our results to the sponsored search setting. In the standard sponsored search setting, a search engine typically has several slots available for advertisements. These slots have different CTRs and are sold to interested advertisers via auctions. Each keyword corresponds to an auction. When a user enters a keyword query, the search engine collects bids from the bidders that are interested in this keyword, and allocates the slots to the winning bidders. If the user clicks on an advertisement, the corresponding advertiser pays according to some payment rules.

Assume that there are K available slots and the j-th slot has a CTR s_j satisfying $s_1 \geqslant s_2 \geqslant \cdots \geqslant s_K \geqslant 0$. There are N bidders and our mechanism computes for each bidder i a ranking score $R_i(v_i) = \alpha P(v_i) + (1 - \alpha)Q(\varphi_i(v_i))$, then allocates the j-th slot to the bidder with the j-th highest score. We show that both the welfare and the revenue of our mechanism are monotone with respect to α.

Even though the K identical items setting and the sponsored search setting both belong to the "single-parameter" setting, the analysis from the previous subsection cannot be directly applied here since in this setting, different slots have different CTRs, i.e., slots are not identical. We overcome this technical difficulty by decomposing the sponsored search auctions into K sub-auctions with the j-th sub-auction selling j identical slots. Then our results in previous sections still hold for each sub-auction. We aggregate the results for the sub-auctions together to show that they can be extended to this setting.

Theorem 4.3   *Let $P(\cdot)$ and $Q(\cdot)$ be two increasing functions. Suppose there are K slots with CTRs $s_1 \geqslant s_2 \geqslant \cdots \geqslant s_K \geqslant 0$ and* *the distributions F_i that each bidder's valuation is drawn from satisfies the regularity condition. Then $\mathrm{REV}(\mathcal{M}(\alpha, r))$ is monotone decreasing in α while $\mathrm{WEL}(\mathcal{M}(\alpha, r))$ is monotone increasing in α.*

Proof Let $s_{K+1} = 0$ and $x^{(\alpha)}$ be the allocation rule of the mechanism $\mathcal{M}(\alpha, r)$. Note that only pointing out whether a bidder is a winner is not enough in this setting, since the slots have different CTRs. So we let $x_i^{(\alpha)} \in \{s_i | 1 \leqslant i \leqslant K+1\}$ to specify the slot that is allocated to bidder i. If bidder i loses in the auction, we say that i wins the $(K+1)$-th slot and $x_i^{(\alpha)} = s_{K+1} = 0$. Thus the welfare and revenue can be written as:

$$\mathrm{WEL}(\mathcal{M}(\alpha, r)) = \mathrm{E}_{v \sim F(v)} \left[\sum_{i=1}^{N} x_i^{(\alpha)} v_i \right],$$

$$\mathrm{REV}(\mathcal{M}(\alpha, r)) = \mathrm{E}_{v \sim F(v)} \left[\sum_{i=1}^{N} x_i^{(\alpha)} \varphi_i(v_i) \right]$$

Let $d_j = s_j - s_{j+1} \geqslant 0, \forall 1 \leqslant j < K$. We decompose the auction into K sub-auctions with the j-th $(1 \leqslant j \leqslant K)$ auction selling the first j slots to N bidders. In the j-th sub-auction, all the j slots for sale have the same CTR of d_j. Thus the j-th sub-auction actually sells j identical items. We apply our mechanism $\mathcal{M}(\alpha, r)$ to these K sub-auctions, i.e., in the j-th sub-auction, we compute the ranking score for each bidder, and allocate the slots to the highest j bidders. Denote the j-th sub-auction by $\mathcal{A}^{(j)}(\alpha, r)$ and let $x_i^{(j,\alpha)} \in \{0, 1\}$ be its allocation rule. Clearly, for any $j > l$, winners of $\mathcal{A}^{(l)}(\alpha, r)$ are also winners of $\mathcal{A}^{(j)}(\alpha, r)$. And if a bidder i wins the l-th $(1 \leqslant l \leqslant K)$ slot in the original auction, then i is also among the winners of sub-auctions $j \geqslant l$. Thus we have that for all i,

$$\sum_{j=1}^{K} d_j x_i^{(j,\alpha)} = \sum_{j=1}^{l-1} d_j \cdot 0 + \sum_{j=l}^{K} d_j \cdot 1 = \sum_{j=l}^{K} s_j - s_{j+1} = s_l = x_i^{(\alpha)} \quad (4.7)$$

Now consider each sub-auction $\mathcal{A}^{(j)}(\alpha, r)$. For any $0 \leqslant \alpha_1 < \alpha_2 \leqslant 1$, according to Theorem 4.1,

$$\sum_{i=1}^{N} x_i^{(j,\alpha_1)} \varphi_i(v_i) \geqslant \sum_{i=1}^{N} x_i^{(j,\alpha_2)} \varphi_i(v_i),$$

$$\sum_{i=1}^{N} x_i^{(j,\alpha_1)} v_i \leqslant \sum_{i=1}^{N} x_i^{(j,\alpha_2)} v_i$$

Multiply the above inequalities by d_j and sum over j, and we obtain:

$$\sum_{j=1}^{K} d_j \left(\sum_{i=1}^{N} x_i^{(j,\alpha_1)} \varphi_i(v_i) \right) \geqslant \sum_{j=1}^{K} d_j \left(\sum_{i=1}^{N} x_i^{(j,\alpha_2)} \varphi_i(v_i) \right),$$

$$\sum_{j=1}^{K} d_j \left(\sum_{i=1}^{N} x_i^{(j,\alpha_1)} v_i \right) \leqslant \sum_{j=1}^{K} d_j \left(\sum_{i=1}^{N} x_i^{(j,\alpha_2)} v_i \right)$$

Switching the order of summation and applying equation (4.7) gives

$$\sum_{i=1}^{N} \varphi_i(v_i) x_i^{(\alpha_1)} \geqslant \sum_{i=1}^{N} \varphi_i(v_i) x_i^{(\alpha_2)},$$

$$\sum_{i=1}^{N} v_i x_i^{(\alpha_1)} \leqslant \sum_{i=1}^{N} v_i x_i^{(\alpha_2)}$$

Taking expectation yields:

$$\mathrm{REV}(\mathcal{M}(\alpha_1, r)) \geqslant \mathrm{REV}(\mathcal{M}(\alpha_2, r)),$$

$$\mathrm{WEL}(\mathcal{M}(\alpha_1, r)) \leqslant \mathrm{WEL}(\mathcal{M}(\alpha_2, r))$$

completing the proof since the above inequalities hold for all $0 \leqslant \alpha_1 < \alpha_2 \leqslant 1$.

The following result generalizes Theorem 4.2.

Theorem 4.4   *Let $P(\cdot)$ and $Q(\cdot)$ be two functions that are increasing, concave and differentiable, and there exists a constant $c > 0$ such that $Q'(t) \geqslant cP'(t) > 0, \forall t$. Suppose there are K slots with CTRs $s_1 \geqslant s_2 \geqslant \cdots \geqslant s_K \geqslant 0$ and the distributions F_i satisfies the monotone hazard rate condition for all i. Let r^* be the Myerson reserve price profile for the bidders. Then $\mathrm{REV}(\mathcal{M}(\alpha, r^*))$ is a $(2 - \theta)$-approximation of the optimal mechanism, where $\theta = \dfrac{(1 - \alpha)c}{\alpha + (1 - \alpha)c}$.*

Proof   We also decompose the original auction into K sub-auctions and follow the notations defined in the proof of Theorem 4.3.   Let

$x^{(OPT)}$ be the allocation function of the original auction and $x^{(j,OPT)} \in \{0,1\}(1 \leqslant j \leqslant K)$ be the allocation function of the corresponding j-th sub-auction. It is clear that for each bidder i,

$$x_i^{(OPT)} = \sum_{j=1}^{K} d_j x_i^{(j,OPT)}$$

And from Theorem 4.2, we have that for each sub-auction j:

$$(2-\theta) \sum_{i=1}^{N} \varphi_i(v_i) x_i^{(j,\alpha)} \geqslant \sum_{i=1}^{N} \varphi_i(v_i) x_i^{(j,OPT)}$$

Multiply the above inequality by d_j and sum over all sub-auctions j and we have

$$(2-\theta) \sum_{j=1}^{K} d_j \left(\sum_{i=1}^{N} \varphi_i(v_i) x_i^{(j,\alpha)} \right) \geqslant \sum_{j=1}^{K} d_j \left(\sum_{i=1}^{N} \varphi_i(v_i) x_i^{(j,OPT)} \right)$$

Applying the fact $x_i^{(\alpha)} = \sum_{j=1}^{K} d_j x_i^{(j,\alpha)}$ gives

$$(2-\theta) \sum_{i=1}^{N} \varphi_i(v_i) x_i^{(\alpha)} \geqslant \sum_{i=1}^{N} \varphi_i(v_i) x_i^{(OPT)}$$

Taking expectation over v yields

$$(2-\theta)\text{Rev}(\mathcal{M}(\alpha, r^*)) \geqslant \text{Rev}(OPT)$$

completing the proof.

4.1.4　Experiments

In Theorem 4.1, we show that in the "K identical items" setting, both the welfare and revenue of our mechanism are monotone with respect to the parameter α.

To verify our results, we first consider a relatively simple case. We assume that there are 3 identical items for sale and 10 interested bidders. The value of bidder i is uniformly distributed in the interval $[0, u_i]$, where u_i is again uniformly distributed in the interval[1-2]. No reserve prices are set for all bidders. We set the functions $P(t) = Q(t) = t$ and $c = 1$, so the only parameter in the simulation is α. The numbers in the figures are normalized since the absolute value is not important.

Figure 4.1(a) shows that the welfare changes almost linearly with respect to α within a large range of values. The revenue, however, changes slowly when α is small and rapidly when α is large. Therefore we can set an appropriate α value to achieve a great welfare gain but only suffer from a slight revenue loss.

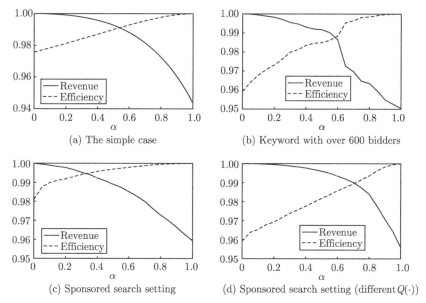

Figure 4.1 Revenue vs. Efficiency

We also evaluate our mechanisms in the sponsored search setting. We use real data from one of the major search engines in Chinese. We first select a keyword with over 600 bidders. There are 3 slots for sale, with the first slots having a CTR of about 0.1. We extract two weeks' data for the keyword. Each bidder's valuations for the keyword is fitted to a lognormal distribution[①], and assume that these bidders have independent distributions. Then we run the auction 1000 times. Inside

---

① Note that the lognormal distribution does not satisfy the regularity condition. Nevertheless, the simulation is complementary to our theoretical results, showing that our mechanism works under this setting as well.

each auction, we draw a sample bid for each bidder according to their respective distributions, and allocate the 3 slots based on our ranking algorithm. We use the average welfare and revenue of the 1000 auctions as the per-impression welfare and revenue. We still choose $P(t) = Q(t) = t$ and $c = 1$ for this simulation but use the monopoly reserve price for each bidder. Figure 4.1(b) shows similar trends as in the simple case.

Next, we evaluate our mechanism on the most profitable 100 keywords. Each keyword has nearly 500 interested bidders on average and the most popular has over 1500 bidders. We adopt the same simulation method as described above for each keyword. After computing the per-impression welfare and revenue of these 100 keywords, we multiply them by their respective occurrence frequency and then add them together to compute the total welfare and revenue.

Figure 4.1(c) shows that the welfare is sensitive with respect to α (changes quickly) when α is small, which may cause some inconvenience for parameter tuning if the objective is to guarantee a certain amount of welfare. However, this problem could be solved by simply changing the function $Q(t) = t$ to $Q(t) = \frac{0.5}{1.2}t^{1.2} + \frac{0.5}{0.8}t^{0.8}$. It is clear that we still have $Q'(t) \geqslant 1, \forall t > 0$. This ranking algorithm causes the welfare to change almost linearly (shown in Figure 4.1(d)), making it easier to tune the parameter α.

4.2   Balancing Objectives through Machine Learning[①]

In this section, we study how to make use of machine learning algorithms to tradeoff between different objectives. The problem of market clearing is to set a price for an item such that the quantity demanded equals the quantity supplied. We cast the problem of predicting clearing prices into a learning framework and use the resulting models to perform revenue optimization in auctions and markets with

① This section was originally published as reference [28]: Weiran Shen, Sébastien Lahaie, Renato Paes Leme. Learning to Clear the Market[C]//Proceedings of the 36th International Conference on Machine Learning, 2019: 5710-5718.

contextual information. The economic intuition behind market clearing allows us to obtain fine-grained control over the aggressiveness of the resulting pricing policy, grounded in theory. To evaluate our approach, we fit a model of clearing prices over a massive dataset of bids in display ad auctions from a major ad exchange. The learned prices outperform other modeling techniques in the literature in terms of revenue and efficiency trade-offs. Because of the convex nature of the clearing loss function, the convergence rate of our method is as fast as linear regression.

4.2.1 Background

A key difficulty in designing machine learning systems for revenue optimization in auctions and markets is the discontinuous nature of the problem. Consider the basic problem of setting a reserve price in a single-item auction (e.g., for online advertising): revenue steadily increases with the price up to the point where all buyers drop out, at which point it suddenly drops to zero. The discontinuity may average away over a large market, but one is typically left with a highly non-convex objective function, which is difficult to optimize.

We are interested in obtaining pricing policies for revenue optimization in a data-rich (i.e., contextual) environment, where each product is associated with a set of features. For example, in online display advertising, a product is an ad impression (an ad placement viewed by the user) which is annotated with features like geo-information, device type, cookies, etc. There are two main approaches to reserve pricing in this domain: one is to divide the feature space into well-defined clusters and apply a traditional (non-contextual) revenue optimization algorithm in each cluster[2, 29-31]. This is effectively a semi-parametric approach with the drawback that an overly fine clustering leads to data sparsity and the inability to learn across clusters. An overly coarse clustering, on the other hand, does not fully take advantage of the rich features available.

To overcome these difficulties, a natural alternative is to fit a parametric pricing policy by optimizing a loss function. The first instinct is to use revenue itself as a loss function, but this loss is notoriously difficult to optimize because it is discontinuous, non-convex, and has zero gradient over much of its domain—so one must look to surrogates.

Median and Mohri[32] propose a continuous surrogate loss for revenue whose gradient information is rich enough to optimize for prices. The loss is nevertheless non-convex so optimizing it relies on techniques from constrained DC-programming, which have provable convergence but limited scalability in high-dimensional contexts.

4.2.1.1　Main Contributions

The main innovation in our framework is to address the revenue optimization problem by instead looking to the closely related problem of market clearing: how to set prices so that demand equals supply. The loss function for market clearing exhibits several nice properties from a learning perspective, notably convexity. The market clearing objective dates back to the economic theory of market equilibrium[33], and more recently arises in the literature on iterative auctions[34-36]. To our knowledge, our work is the first to use it as a loss function in a machine-learning context.

The economic insight behind the market-clearing loss function allows us to adapt its shape to control how conservative or aggressive the resulting prices are in extracting revenue. To increase price levels, we can artificially increase demand or limit supply, which connects revenue optimization theorems from computational economics[37-38] to regularization techniques under our loss function.

We begin by casting the problem of market clearing as a learning problem. Given a dataset where each record corresponds to an item characterized by a feature vector, together with buyer bids and the seller asks for the item, the goal of the pricing policy is to quote a price that balances supply and demand; with a single seller, this simply means predicting a price in between the highest- and second-highest bids, which intuitively improves over the baseline of no reserve pricing.

This offers us a general framework for price optimization in contextual settings, but the objective function of market clearing is still disconnected from revenue optimization. Revenue is the aggregate price paid by buyers, while market clearing is linked to the problem of optimizing efficiency (realized value). Efficiency can be measured as social welfare (the total value of the allocated items), or more coarsely via the match rate (the number of cleared transactions). The platform faces a tension between trying to extract as much revenue as possible from buyers, while also leaving them enough surplus to discourage a move to competing platforms.

To better understand the trade-off between revenue and efficiency, we consider the linear programming duality between allocation and pricing and observe that a natural parameter that trades-off revenue for efficiency is the available supply. Artificially limiting supply (or increasing demand) allows one to control the aggressiveness of the resulting clearing prices output by the model. This fundamental idea has been used multiple times more recently in algorithmic game theory to design approximately revenue-optimal auctions[15, 29, 38, 39]. Translating this intuition to our setting, a simple modification of the primal (allocation) linear program has the effect of restricting the supply. In the dual (pricing) linear program, this is equivalent to adding a regularization to the market-clearing objective function.

The focus of this work is empirical. As our main application, we use this methodology to optimize reserve prices in display advertising auctions. We demonstrate the efficacy of the market clearing loss for reserve pricing by experimentally comparing it with other strategies on a real-world data set. Coupled with the experimental evaluation, we establish some theoretical guarantees on match rate and efficiency for the optimal pricing policy under clearing loss. The theory provides guidance on how to set the regularization parameters and we investigate how this translates to the desired trade-offs experimentally.

4.2.1.2   Experimental Results

We evaluate our method against a linear-regression-based approach on a dataset consisting of over 200M auction records from a major display advertising exchange. The features are represented as 84K-dimensional sparse vectors and contain information such as the website on which the ad will be displayed, device and browser type, and country of origin. As benchmarks, we consider the standard linear regression on either the highest or second-highest bid, and models fit using the surrogate revenue loss proposed by Medina and Mohri[32]. We find that our method Pareto-dominates the benchmarks in terms of the trade-off between revenue and match rate or social welfare. For example, for the best revenue obtained from the regression approach, we can obtain a pricing function with at least the same revenue but a 5% higher social welfare and 10% higher match rate. We also find that the convergence rate of fitting models under our loss function is as fast as a standard linear regression. In comparison, the surrogate loss of Medina and Mohri[32] has much slower convergence due to its non-convexity.

4.2.1.3　Related Works

There is a large body of literature on learning algorithms for optimizing revenue, however, most of the literature deals with the non-contextual setting. Cole and Roughgarden[40], Morgenstern and Roughgarden[41-42] and Paes Leme et al.[31] study the batch-learning non-contextual problem. Roughgarden and Wang[30] study the non-contextual problem both in the online and batch learning settings. Cesa-Bianchi et al.[43] study it as a non-contextual online learning problem. Finally, there has been a lot of recent interest in the contextual online learning version[44-46], but those ideas are not applicable to the batch-learning setting.

Closest to our work are Medina and Mohri[32] and Medina and Vassilvitskii[47], who also study contextual reserve price optimization in a batch-learning setting. Medina and Mohri[32] prove generalization bounds, defines a surrogate loss as a continuous approximation to the revenue loss, and propose an algorithm with provable convergence based on DC programming. The algorithm, however, requires solving a convex program in each iteration. Medina and Vassilvitskii[47] propose a clustering-based approach, which involves the following steps: learning a least-square predictor of the bid, clustering the feature space based on the linear predictor, and optimizing the reserve using a non-contextual method in each cluster.

4.2.2　Market Clearing Loss

This section introduces our model, proceeding from the general to the specific. We first explain the duality between allocation and pricing, which motivates the form of the loss function to fit clearing prices, and provides useful economic insights into how the input data defines its shape. We next define the formal problem of learning a clearing price function in an environment with several buyers and sellers. We then specialize in a single-item, second-price auction (multiple buyers, single seller).

4.2.2.1　Allocation and Pricing

We consider a market with n buyers and m sellers who aim to trade quantities of an item (e.g., a stock or commodity) among themselves. Each buyer i is defined by a pair (b_i, μ_i) where $b_i \in \mathbb{R}_+$ is a bid price and $\mu_i \in \mathbb{R}_+$ is a quantity. The interpretation is that the buyer is willing to buy up to μ_i units of the item at a price of at most b_i per unit. Similarly, each seller j is defined by a pair (c_j, λ_j) where $c_j \in \mathbb{R}_+$ is an ask price and $\lambda_j \in \mathbb{R}_+$ is the quantity of item the seller can supply. The ask price can be viewed as a cost of production, or as an outside offer available to the seller, so that the seller will decline to sell item units for any price less than its ask.

The allocation problem associated with the market is to determine quantities of the item supplied by the sellers, and consumed by the buyers, so as to maximize the *gains from trade*—value consumed minus cost of production. Formally, let x_i be the quantity bought by buyer i and y_j the quantity sold by seller j. The optimal gains from trade are captured by the (linear) optimization problem:

$$\max_{0 \leqslant x_i \leqslant \mu_i, 0 \leqslant y_j \leqslant \lambda_j} \sum_{i=1}^{n} b_i x_i - \sum_{j=1}^{m} c_j y_j$$

$$\text{s.t.} \quad \sum_{i=1}^{n} x_i = \sum_{j=1}^{m} y_j \tag{4.8}$$

The optimization is straightforward to solve: the highest bid is matched with the lowest ask, and the two agents trade as much as possible with each other. The process repeats until the highest bid falls below the lowest ask. The purpose of the linear programming formulation is to consider its dual, which corresponds to a pricing problem:

$$\min_{p} \sum_{i=1}^{n} \mu_i (b_i - p)_+ + \sum_{j=1}^{m} \lambda_j (p - c_j)_+ \tag{4.9}$$

where $(\cdot)_+$ denotes $\max\{\cdot, 0\}$. The optimal dual solution corresponds to a price that balances demand and supply, which is the central concept in this section.

Definition 4.2 A price p^* is a *clearing price* if, for any optimal solution $(\boldsymbol{x}^*, \boldsymbol{y}^*)$ to the allocation problem, we have

$$x_i^* \in \underset{x_i \in [0, \mu_i]}{\arg\max} \; x_i(b_i - p),$$

$$y_j^* \in \underset{y_j \in [0, \lambda_j]}{\arg\max} \; y_j(p - c_j)$$

for each buyer i and seller j.

In words, a clearing price balances supply and demand by ensuring that, at an optimal allocation, each buyer buys a quantity that maximizes its utility (value minus price), and similarly each seller sells a quantity that maximizes its profit (price minus cost). In the current simple setup with a single item, buyer i will buy μ_i units if $b_i > p$, zero units if $b_i < p$, and is indifferent to the number of units bought at $p = b_i$; similarly for each seller j. However, the concept of clearing prices—where each agent maximizes its utility at the optimal allocation—generalizes too much more complex allocation problems with multiple differentiated items and nonlinear valuations over bundles of items[34].

The fact that a clearing price exists, and can be obtained by solving (4.9), follows from standard LP duality. The complementary slackness conditions relating optimal primal solution $(\boldsymbol{x}^*, \boldsymbol{y}^*)$ to optimal dual solution p^* amount to the conditions of Definition 4.2. The optimal solution p^* to the dual corresponds to a Lagrange multiplier for constraint (4.8) which equates to demand and supply.

4.2.2.2 Learning Formulation

To cast market clearing in a learning context, we consider a generic feature space $\mathcal{Z}$ with the label space $\mathcal{T} = \mathbb{R}_+^n \times \mathbb{R}_+^m$ consisting of bid and ask vectors $(\boldsymbol{b}, \boldsymbol{c})$. For the sake of simplicity, we develop our framework assuming that the number of buyers and sellers remains fixed (at n and m), and that the item quantity that each agent demands or supplies (μ_i or λ_j) is also fixed. This information is straightforward to incorporate into the label space if needed, and our results can be adapted accordingly. The objective is to fit a price predictor (also called a pricing policy)

$p : \mathcal{Z} \to \mathbb{R}$ to a training set of data $\{(z_k, \boldsymbol{b}_k, \boldsymbol{c}_k)\}$ drawn from $\mathcal{Z} \times \mathcal{T}$, to achieve good prediction performance on separate test data drawn from the same distribution.

As a concrete example, the training data could consist of bids and asks for a stock on a financial exchange, and the features might be recent economic data on the company, time of day or week, etc. The clearing problem here is equivalent to predicting a price within each datapoint's bid-ask spread given the features. As another example, the data could consist of bids for ad impressions on a display ad exchange, and the features might be contextual information about the website (e.g., topic) and user (e.g., whether she is on mobile or desktop). The clearing problem there reduces to predicting a price between the highest and second-highest bids.

Based on our developments so far, the correct loss function to fit clearing prices is given by expression(4.9), which we call the *clearing loss*:

$$\ell^c(p, z, \boldsymbol{b}, \boldsymbol{c}) = \sum_{i=1}^{n} \mu_i (b_i - p(z))_+ + \sum_{j=1}^{m} \lambda_j (p(z) - c_j)_+$$

Figure 4.2 illustrates the shape of the clearing loss (in green) under an instance with buyers $(\$1, 1)$, $(\$4, 1)$, $(\$5, 2)$, and sellers $(\$2, 1)$, $(\$3, 1)$. Here any price between \$4 and \$5 is a clearing price. If we add an extra buyer $(\$6, 1)$, the loss curve tilts to the right (in blue) and the unique clearing price becomes \$5; since there is more demand, the clearing price increases. If we instead add an extra seller $(\$2, 2)$, the curve tilts to the left (in pink), and the clearing price decreases. This example hints at a way to control the aggressiveness of the price function p fit to the data, by artificially adjusting demand or supply.

Over a training set of data $\{(z_k, \boldsymbol{b}_k, \boldsymbol{c}_k)\}$, model fitting consists of computing a pricing policy p that minimizes the overall loss $\sum_k \ell^c(p, z_k, \boldsymbol{b}_k, \boldsymbol{c}_k)$. Under a limited number of contexts z_k, it may be possible to directly compute optimal clearing prices, or even revenue-maximizing reserve prices, based on the bid distributions in each context [2, 40]. But this kind of nonparametric approach quickly runs into difficulties when there is a large number of contexts or even continuous features, where issues of data sparsity and discretization arise. Our formulation allows one to impose some structure on the pricing policy (e.g., a linear model or neural net) whenever this aids with generalization.

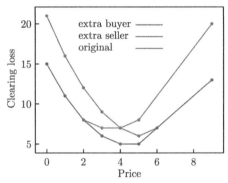

Figure 4.2   **Effect on the shape of the clearing loss when adding a buyer or a seller (see the color figure before)**

From a learning perspective, clearing loss has several attractive properties. It is a piece-wise linear convex function, where the kink locations are determined by the bids and asks. The magnitude of its derivatives depends only on the buyer and seller quantities, which makes it robust to any outliers in the bids or asks. By its derivation via LP duality, its optimal value equals the optimal gains from trade, which are easy to compute. This gives a reference point to quantify how well a price function fits any given dataset.

4.2.2.3   Reserve Pricing

As a practical application of the clearing loss, we consider the problem of reserve pricing in a single-item, second-price auction. In this setting, every buyer demands a single unit ($\mu_i = 1$), and there is a single seller ($m = 1$) with cost c. The seller also has unit supply, but we still parametrize its quantity by λ to allow some control on the shape of the loss.

We write $b^{(1)}$ and $b^{(2)}$ to denote the highest and second-highest bids, respectively. In a single-item second-price auction, the item is allocated to the highest bidder as long as $b^{(1)} \geqslant c$, and is charged $\bar{c} \equiv \max\{b^{(2)}, c\}$. Second-price auctions are extremely common and until now have been the dominant format for selling display ads online through ad exchanges, among countless other applications. It is common for the seller to set a *reserve price*, a minimum price that the winning bidder is charged. The cost c is itself a reserve price, but the seller may choose to increase this to some price p in an attempt to extract more revenue, at the risk of leaving the item unsold if it turns out that $b^{(1)} < p$. Revenue as a function of p can be negated to define a loss, which we denote ℓ^r:

$$-\ell^r(p, z, \boldsymbol{b}, c) = \begin{cases} \max\{p(z), \bar{c}\}, & \max\{p(z), c\} \leqslant b^{(1)} \\ c, & \text{otherwise} \end{cases}$$

However, this loss is notoriously difficult to optimize directly, because it is non-convex and even discontinuous, and its gradient is 0 except over a possibly narrow range between the highest and second-highest bids. Clearing loss represents a promising alternative for reserve pricing because any price between $\bar{c}$ and $b^{(1)}$ is a clearing price, so a correct clearing price prediction should intuitively improve over the baseline of c. The clearing loss in the auction setting takes the form:

$$\ell^c(p, z, \boldsymbol{b}, c) = \sum_{i=1}^{n} (b_i - p(z))_+ + \lambda(p(z) - c)_+ \tag{4.10}$$

In practical applications of reserve pricing it is often desirable to achieve some degree of control over the *match rate*—the fraction of auctions where the item is sold—and the closely related metric of *social welfare*—the aggregate value of the items sold, where value is captured by the winning bid $b^{(1)}$. Formally, these concepts are defined as follows, where the notation $[\![\cdot]\!]$ is 1 if its predicate is true and 0 otherwise.

Definition 4.3 On a single data point, the *match rate* at price p is $\mathsf{MR}(p) = [\![b^{(1)} \geqslant \max\{p, c\}]\!]$ and the *social welfare* is $\mathsf{SW}(p) = b^{(1)}[\![b^{(1)} \geqslant \max\{p, c\}]\!]$.

As with the revenue objective, match rate and social welfare are discontinuous and their gradients are almost everywhere 0, so they are not directly suitable for model fitting via convex optimization (i.e., one has to look to surrogates).

Note that the clearing loss (4.10) effectively contains a term that approximately regularizes according to the match rate. The seller's term $(p - c)_+$ can be viewed as a hinge-type surrogate for the match rate, since any setting of p above c risks impacting the match rate. Increasing

λ improves the match rate, in line with the earlier economic intuition that increasing seller supply λ shifts the clearing price downwards. Symmetrically, λ can be decreased within the range $[0, 1]$ (the loss remains convex in this range), which is equivalent to increasing each buyer's demand to $\mu = 1/\lambda$. According to the economic intuition, this shifts the clearing price upwards at the expense of the match rate. The fact that the relevant range and units of the regularization weight λ are understood is very convenient in practice. In the next section, we derive a quantitative link between λ and the match rate.

4.2.3 Theoretical Guarantees

In this section, we prove approximation guarantees on the match rate and efficiency performance of models fit using the clearing loss. The results will provide guidelines for setting the regularization parameters for fine-grained control of the match rate.

We begin by characterizing the optimal pricing policy under clearing loss when there is no restriction on the policy structure, assuming that bids and costs are drawn independently (but not necessarily identically).

Theorem 4.5 *If conditioned on each feature vector z the bid and cost distributions are given by $b_i \sim F_i^z$ and $c_j \sim G_j^z$, then the pricing policy that optimizes clearing loss is the solution to*

$$\sum_i \mu_i(1 - F_i^z(p(z))) = \sum_j \lambda_j G_j^z(p(z))$$

which is the policy that balances expected supply and demand.

Proof We can write the expectation of the market clearing loss function as follows:

$$\mathrm{E}[\ell^c(p)] = \sum_{i=1}^{n} \mu_i \int_p^{\infty} (b_i - p) \, \mathrm{d}F_i^z(b_i) + \sum_{j=1}^{m} \lambda_j \int_0^p (p - c_j) \, \mathrm{d}G_j^z(c_j)$$

Taking the derivative with respect to p and setting it to zero leads to:

$$0 = \frac{\mathrm{d}}{\mathrm{d}p} \mathrm{E}[\ell^c(p)] = -\sum_{i=1}^{n} \mu_i(1 - F_i^z(p)) + \sum_{j=1}^{m} \lambda_j G_j^z(p)$$

which immediately leads to the equation in the theorem.

We now consider the single-item auction setting where $m = 1$ and $\mu_i = 1$ for all buyers. For simplicity, also assume that $c = 0$, which implies $G_j(p) = 1$ for all p. In that case, we can bound the match rate by a simple formula.

Theorem 4.6   *In the setup with a single seller with λ supply and cost $c = 0$, and independent buyer distributions, the expected match rate under the optimal clearing price policy is at least $1 - e^{-\lambda}$.*

Proof   A transaction clears if there is at least one buyer with a valuation above the price p which happens with probability $1 - \prod_{i=1}^{n} F_i^z(p)$. Since the optimal policy p is the solution to $\sum_{i=1}^{n}(1 - F_i^z(p)) = \lambda$ by the previous proposition, we have

$$\mathrm{E}[\mathrm{MR}] = 1 - \prod_{i=1}^{n} F_i^z(p) \geqslant 1 - \left[\frac{1}{n}\sum_{i=1}^{n} F_i^z(p)\right]^n = 1 - \left[1 - \frac{\lambda}{n}\right]^n \geqslant 1 - e^{-\lambda}$$

where the first inequality follows from the arithmetic-geometric mean inequality.

The preceding proposition provides a useful guideline on how to set the regularization parameter λ to achieve a certain target match rate. We can also obtain a similar bound for social welfare:

Corollary 4.2   *In the setting of the previous proposition, the social welfare $\mathrm{E}[\mathrm{SW}] = \mathrm{E}[b^{(1)} \cdot [\![b^{(1)} \geqslant p]\!]]$ obtained by the optimal clearing price policy is at least $1 - e^{-\lambda}$ of optimal social welfare, obtained by setting no reserves.*

Proof   This follows from the fact that $\mathrm{E}[b^{(1)} \cdot [\![b^{(1)} \geqslant p]\!]] \geqslant \mathrm{E}[b^{(1)}] \cdot \mathbb{P}[b^{(1)} \geqslant p] \geqslant (1 - e^{-\lambda}) \cdot \mathrm{E}[b^{(1)}]$.

Another interesting corollary is that when buyers are i.i.d., fitting a clearing price is equivalent to fitting a certain quantile of the common bid distribution.

Corollary 4.3   *In the setup of the previous proposition with i.i.d. buyers, the optimal clearing price policy is to set the price at $p(z) = F^{-1}(1 - \lambda/n)$ where $F = F_i^z$.*

This result makes explicit how varying λ in the clearing loss tunes the aggressiveness of the resulting price function, by moving up or down the quantiles of the bid distribution. In particular, it's possible to span all quantiles using $\lambda \in [0, +\infty]$. Fitting clearing prices is not exactly equivalent to quantile regression, since the relevant quantile depends on the number of buyers, which is a property of the data and not fixed in advance.

4.2.4　Empirical Evaluation

In this section, we evaluate our approach of using predicted clearing prices as a reserve pricing policy in second-price auctions. We collected a dataset of auction records by sampling a fraction of the logs from Google's Ad Exchange over two consecutive days in January 2019. Our sample contains over 100M records for each day. In display advertising, online publishers (e.g., websites like nytimes.com) can choose to request an ad from an exchange when a user visits a page on their site. The exchange runs a second-price auction (the most common auction format) among eligible advertisers, possibly with a reserve price.

We clip bid vectors to the top 5 bids. As for the publisher cost c, we use a reserve price available in the data which is meant to capture the opportunity cost[1] of not showing ads from other sources besides the exchange, in line with our model.[2] Reserve prices are only relevant conditional on the top bid exceeding the publisher cost, so the auction records were filtered to satisfy this condition. When reporting our results this means that the baseline match rate without any reserve pricing is 100%, so we will refer to it as the *relative* match rate in our plots and analyses to emphasize this fact.

All the models we evaluate[3] are linear models of the price p as a

---

[1] A common alternative source of display ads besides exchanges are reservation contracts, which are advertiser-publisher agreements to show a fixed volume of ads for a time period. If the contract is not fulfilled, this comes at a penalty to the publisher.

[2] We also excluded additional sources of reserve prices from the dataset: (a) reserve prices configured by publishers reflecting business objectives like avoiding channel conflict (i.e., protecting the value of inventory sold through other means) and (b) automated reserve prices set by the exchange.

[3] We evaluate the models by simulating the effect of the new reserve prices on a test dataset. The simulation does not take into account possible strategic responses on the part of buyers. However, since the auction format is a second price auction, it is a dominant strategy for the buyers to always bid truthfully.

function of features z of the auction records. The only difference between the models is the loss function used to fit each one, to focus on the impact of the choice of the loss function. The features we used included: publisher id, device type (mobile, desktop, tablet), OS type (e.g., Android or iOS), country, and format (video or display). For sparse features like publisher id, we used a one-hot encoding for the most common ids and an 'other' bucket for ids in the tail. The models were all fit using TensorFlow with the default Adam optimizer and minibatches of size 512 distributed over 20 machines. An iteration corresponds to one minibatch update in each machine, therefore 20×512 data points. The models were all trained over at least 400K iterations, although for some models convergence occurred much earlier.

Besides the clearing loss, we considered several other losses as benchmarks:

- Least-squares regression on the highest bid $b^{(1)}$.
- Least-squares regression on the 2nd-highest bid $b^{(2)}$.
- A revenue surrogate loss function proposed by Medina and Mohri[32] as a continuous alternative to the pure revenue loss ℓ^r mentioned previously:

$$-\ell^\gamma(p, z, \boldsymbol{b}, c) = \begin{cases} \max\{p(z), \bar{c}\}, & p(x) \leqslant b_1 \\ c, & p(x) > (1 + \gamma)b_1 \\ ((1 + \gamma)b_1 - p(x))/\gamma, & \text{otherwise} \end{cases}$$

The loss has a free parameter $\gamma > 0$ which can be tuned to control the approximation to ℓ^r. Although this loss is continuous, it is still non-convex. In our experiments we tried a range of $\gamma \in \{0.25, 0.5, 0.75, 1\}$. Below we report on the setting $\gamma = 0.75$ which gave the best revenue performance.

For each loss function we added the match-rate regularization $\lambda(p - c)_+$, and varied λ to span a range of realized match rates. Recall that this is already implicit in the clearing loss, where λ can be construed as the item quantity supplied by the seller. We used non-negative λ to ensure that convexity is preserved if the original loss is itself convex.

We used the first day of data as the training set and the second day as the test set. The performance was very similar on both for all fitted models, which is expected due to the volume of data and the generalization properties of this learning problem[41]. We report results over the test set below.

4.2.4.1　Revenue Performance

We first consider the revenue performance of the different losses as it trades off against match rate and buyer welfare. Figure 4.3 plots the ratio of realized revenue with learned reserves against the realized match rate (Figure 4.3(a)). Both axes are normalized by the revenue and match rate of the second price auction using only the seller's cost as reserves. Each point represents a pair of revenue and match rate or welfare achieved at a certain setting λ. The most immediate observation is that the curve traced out by the clearing loss Pareto dominates the performance of the benchmark loss functions, in the sense that for any fixed match rate, the clearing loss' revenue performance lies higher than the others. The best revenue performance is a 20% improvement achieved by the clearing loss at $\lambda = 0.25$ with a match rate of 30%.

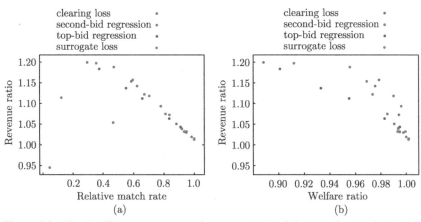

Figure 4.3　Trade-off between revenue improvement and decrease in match rate (a) or buyer welfare (b) (see the color figure before)

Each point represents the performance of the fitted model under a loss function for a fixed regularization level

We also plot in the figure the revenue against welfare (Figure 4.3(b)). We again normalize each axis by the revenue and welfare of the auction that uses only the seller's costs (which achieves the optimal social welfare). For the sake of clarity, the range of the x-axis has been clipped. The Pareto dominance here is even more pronounced, and it's also striking to note that clearing loss can achieve revenue improvements of over 10% with less than 2% impact on buyer welfare.

Another interesting aspect of Figure 4.3 is the range of match rates spanned by the different losses. Recall that, under the assumptions and results of Proposition 4.6, varying λ from 0 to large values should allow the clearing loss to span the full range of match rates in $(0, 1)$, and this is borne out by the plot. For the regressions on $b^{(1)}$ and $b^{(2)}$, there is a hard floor on the match rate that they can achieve with $\lambda = 0$, respectively at 0.38 and 0.67. Another kind of regularization term would be needed to push these further downward and reach more aggressive prices. The match rate for the surrogate loss was particularly sensitive to regularization. Over a range of λ spanning from 0 to 1, only $\lambda = 0$ and $\lambda = 0.1$ yielded match rates below 1, at 0.47 and 0.92 respectively.

4.2.4.2   Controlling the Match Rate

In practice setting the right regularization weight λ to achieve a target match rate is usually the process of trial and error, even to determine the relevant range to inspect, and this was the case for all the benchmark losses. For the clearing loss, however, Proposition 4.6 gives a link between the match rate and λ which can serve as a guide. Specifically, the result prescribes $\lambda = \lg\left(\dfrac{1}{1 - \mathsf{MR}}\right)$ to achieve a match rate of MR.

Figure 4.4 plots the target match rate implied by the settings of λ that we used, according to this formula, against realized match rates. The vertical line shows the reference point of $\lambda = 1$, which is the "default" form of the clearing loss without artificially increasing or limiting supply, with an associated match rate $1 - 1/\mathrm{e} \approx 0.63$. The realized match rate tracks the target fairly well but not perfectly. A possible reason for the discrepancy is that the assumption of i.i.d. bidders that the formula relies on may not hold in practice. Another possible reason is that the linear model may not be expressive enough to fit the optimal price level within each feature context z.

Interestingly, the target match rate from Proposition 4.6 tracks not only the overall match-rate but also the segment-specific match rate. In

Figure 4.4, we break down the match rates by device type and find that they are very consistent across devices.

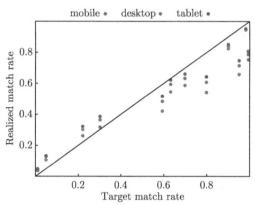

Figure 4.4 Realized match rate against target match rate under the model fit with the clearing loss, broken down by device type (see the color figure before)

The vertical line denotes the parameter setting $\lambda = 1$ with a target match rate of
$$1 - 1/e \approx 0.63$$

4.2.4.3 Convergence Rate

We next consider the convergence rates of model-fitting under the various loss functions, plotted in Figure 4.5. Convergence rates for the clearing loss and the regression losses are very comparable. The main difference between the curves has to do with initialization. Initial prices tended to be high under our random initialization scheme, which is more favorable to regression on the highest bid. All models have converged by 100K iterations. Since square loss is ideal from an optimization perspective, these results imply that models with clearing loss can be fit very quickly and conveniently in practice, in a matter of hours over large display ad datasets. In Figure 4.6 we compare the convergence of the clearing loss with the surrogate loss. Convergence is much slower under surrogate loss. This was expected, as the loss is nonconvex and it has ranges with 0 gradient where the Adam optimizer (or any of the other standard TensorFlow optimizers) cannot make progress; it was nonetheless an important benchmark to evaluate since it closely mimics the true revenue objective. Medina and Mohri[32] discuss alternatives for optimizing the surrogate loss, and propose a special purpose algorithm based on DC-programming (difference of convex functions programming), but they only scale it to thousands of training instances. The fact that the surrogate loss has not quite converged after 400K iterations is a contributing factor to its revenue performance in Figure 4.3.

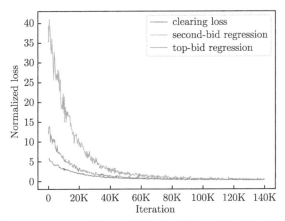

Figure 4.5 Convergence rate of the model under different loss function, in minibatch iterations. We plot the value of each loss across iterations normalized by its value upon convergence (see the color figure before)

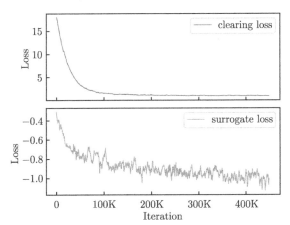

Figure 4.6 Convergence rate of the model under clearing and surrogate function, in minibatch iterations. Both loss functions are smoothed using a 0.9 moving average

4.2.4.4 Effectiveness of Linear Regression

While the key take-away of our empirical evaluation is the fact that the clearing loss dominates other methods in terms of revenue vs.

match rate trade-offs, another surprising consequence of this study is the effectiveness of using a simple regression on the top bid. The natural intuition would be that any least-squares regression should perform poorly since it has the same penalty for underpricing (which is a small loss in revenue) and overpricing (which can cause the transaction to fail and hence incur a large revenue loss). Indeed it is the case that an unregularized regression (the leftmost green point in Figure 4.3) incurs a large match rate loss, but it also achieves significant revenue improvement (albeit with an almost 5% loss in social welfare compared to the clearing loss). Looking into the data, we found that an explanation for this fact is that the bid distributions tend to be highly skewed, which causes standard regression to underpredict for high bids and overpredict for low bids. In fact, under zero regularization, the linear regression on the top bid underpredicts 17.7% of instances for bids below the median and 99.1% for bids above the median. This type of behavior explains why the standard regression can be effective in practice despite the fact that square loss does not encode any difference between underpredicting and overpredicting.

References

[1] SHEN W, TANG P. Practical versus optimal mechanisms[C]//Proceedings of the 16th Conference on Autonomous Agents and MultiAgent Systems. International Foundation for Autonomous Agents and Multiagent Systems, 2017: 78-86.

[2] MYERSON R B. Optimal auction design[J]. Mathematics of Operations Research, 1981, 6(1): 58–73.

[3] MASKIN E, RILEY J, HAHN F. Optimal multi-unit auctions[J]. The Economics of Missing Markets, Information, and Games. 1989.

[4] DENG C, PEKEC S. Money for nothing: exploiting negative externalities[C]//Proceedings of the 12th ACM Conference on Electronic Commerce. ACM, 2011: 361–370.

[5] TANG P, WANG Z. Optimal auctions for negatively correlated items[C]// Proceedings of the 2016 ACM Conference on Economics and Computation. ACM, 2016: 103-120.

[6]   TANG P, WANG Z. Optimal mechanisms with simple menus[J]. Journal of Mathematical Economics, 2017.

[7]   DASKALAKIS C, DECKELBAUM A, TZAMOS C. Strong duality for a multiple-good monopolist[J]. Econometrica, 2017, 85(3): 735–767.

[8]   NISAN N, RONEN A. Algorithmic mechanism design[C]//Proceedings of the Thirty-First Annual ACM Symposium on Theory of Computing. ACM, 1999: 129–140.

[9]   CONITZER V, SANDHOLM T. Automated mechanism design for a self-interested designer[C]//Proceedings of the 4th ACM Conference on Electronic Commerce. ACM, 2003: 232–233.

[10] EDELMAN B, OSTOVSKY M, SCHWARZ M. Internet advertising and the generalized second-price auction: Selling billions of dollars worth of keywords[J]. The American Economic Review, 2007, 97(1): 242–259.

[11] VARIAN H R. Position auctions[J]. International Journal of Industrial Organization, 2007, 25(6): 1163–1178.

[12] MIRROKNI V, LEME R P, TANG P, et al. Dynamic auctions with bank accounts[C]//Proceedings of the Twenty-Fifth International Joint Conference on Artificial Intelligence.AAAI Press, 2016: 387–393.

[13] TANG P, SANDHOLM T. Optimal auctions for spiteful bidders[C]// Proceedings of the Twenty-Sixth AAAI Conference on Artificial Intelligence. AAAI Press, 2012: 1457–1463.

[14] NEKIPELOV D, SYRGKANIS V, TARDOS E. Econometrics for learning agents[C]//Proceedings of the Sixteenth ACM Conference on Economics and Computation. ACM, 2015: 1–18.

[15] HARTLINE J D, ROUGHGARDEN T. Simple versus optimal mechanisms[C]//Proceedings of the 10th ACM Conference on Electronic Commerce. ACM, 2009: 225-234.

[16] TANG P, SANDHOLM T. Approximating optimal combinatorial auctions for complements using restricted welfare maximization[C]//Proceedings of the Twenty-Second International Joint Conference on Artificial Intelligence. AAAI Press, 2011: 379–385.

[17] CHAWLA S, FU H, KARLIN A. Approximate revenue maximization in interdependent value settings[C]//Proceedings of the Fifteenth ACM Conference on Economics and Computation. ACM, 2014: 277–294.

[18] ALAEI S, FU H, HAGHPANAH N, et al. The simple economics of approximately optimal auctions[C]//2013 IEEE 54th Annual Symposium on Foundations of Computer Science. IEEE, 2013: 628-637.

[19] HUANG Z, MANSOUR Y, ROUGHGARDEN T. Making the most of your samples[C]//Proceedings of the Sixteenth ACM Conference on Economics and Computation. ACM, 2015: 45-60.

[20] LI X, YAO ACC. On revenue maximization for selling multiple independently distributed items[C]//Proceedings of the National Academy of Sciences, 2013, 110(28): 11232-11237.

[21] YAO ACC. An n-to-1 bidder reduction for multi-item auctions and its applications[C]//Proceedings of the twenty-sixth annual ACM-SIAM symposium on Discrete algorithms. Society for Industrial and Applied Mathematics, 2015: 92-109.

[22] ALAEI S, HARTLINE J, NIAZADEH R, et al. Optimal auctions vs. anonymous pricing[J]. Games and Economic Behavior, 2018.

[23] CAI Y, DEVANUR N R, WEINBERG S M. A duality based unified approach to bayesian mechanism design[C]//Proceedings of the Forty-Eighth Annual ACM Symposium on Theory of Computing. ACM, 2016: 926-939.

[24] LAHAIE S, PENNOCK D M. Revenue analysis of a family of ranking rules for keyword auctions[C]//Proceedings of the 8th ACM Conference on Electronic Commerce. ACM, 2007: 50-56.

[25] ROBERTS B, GUNAWARDENA D, KASH I A, et al. Ranking and tradeoffs in sponsored search auctions[C]//Proceedings of the Fourteenth ACM Conference on Electronic Commerce. ACM, 2013: 751-766.

[26] BACHRACH Y, CEPPI SKASH I A, et al. Optimising trade-offs among stakeholders in ad auctions. In Proceedings of the Fifteenth ACM Conference on Economics and Computation. ACM, 2014: 75-92.

[27] PROCACCIA A D, WAJC D, ZHANG H. Approximation-variance tradeoffs in mechanism design[J]. Working Paper, 2016.

[28] SHEN W, LAHAIE S, LEME R P. Learning to clear the market[C]//Proceedings of the 36th International Conference on Machine Learning, 2019.

[29] DHANGWATNOTAI P, ROUGHGARDEN T, YAN Q. Revenue maximization with a single sample[J]. Games and Economic Behavior, 2015, 91: 318-333.

[30] ROUGHGARDEN T, WANG J R. Minimizing regret with multiple reserves[C]//Proceedings of the 2016 ACM Conference on Economics and Computation. ACM, 2016: 601-616.

[31] LEME R P, PÁL M,VASSILVITSKII S. A field guide to personalized reserve prices[C]//Proceedings of the 25th International Conference on World Wide Web. International World Wide Web Conferences Steering Committee, 2016: 1093-1102.

[32] MEDINA A M, MOHRI M. Learning theory and algorithms for revenue optimization in second price auctions with reserve[C]//Proceedings of the 31st International Conference on Machine Learning. 2014: 262–270.

[33] J. ARROW K, DEBREU G. Existence of an equilibrium for a competitive economy[J]. Econometrica, 1954, 22(3): 265–290.

[34] BIKHCHANDAIN S, MAMER J W. Competitive equilibrium in an exchange economy with indivisibilities[J]. Journal of Economic Theory, 1997, 74(2): 385–413.

[35] GUL F, STACCHETTI E. Walrasian equilibrium with gross substitutes[J]. Journal of Economic Theory, 1999, 87(1): 95–124.

[36] AUSUBEL L M. An efficient dynamic auction for heterogeneous commodities[J]. American Economic Review, 2006, 96(3): 602–629.

[37] BULOW J, KLEMPERER P. Auctions versus negotiations[J]. American Economic Review, 1996, 86: 180–194.

[38] ROUGHGARDEN T, TALGAM-COHEN I, YAN Q. Supply-limiting mechanisms[C]//Proceedings of the 13th ACM Conference on Electronic Commerce. ACM, 2012: 844-861.

[39] EDEN A, FELDMAN M, FRIEDLER O, et al. The competition complexity of auctions: A Bulow Klemperer result for multi-dimensional bidders[C]//Proceedings of the 2017 ACM Conference on Economics and Computation. ACM, 2017: 343.

[40] COLE R, ROUGHGARDEN T. The sample complexity of revenue maximization[C]//Proceedings of the 46th annual ACM Symposium on Theory of Computing. ACM, 2014: 243–252.

[41] MORGENSTERN J, ROUGHGARDEN T. On the pseudo-dimension of nearly optimal auctions[C]//Proceedings of the 28th International Conference on Neural Information Processing Systems. MIT Press, 2015: 136–144.

[42] MORGENSTERN J, ROUGHGARDEN T. Learning simple auctions[C]// Proceedings of the Conference on Learning Theory, 2016: 1298–1318.

[43] CESA-BIANCHI N, GENTILE C, MANSOUR Y. Regret minimization for reserve prices in second-price auctions[C]//Proceedings of the Twenty-Fourth Annual ACM-SIAM Symposium on Discrete Algorithms. SIAM, 2013: 1190–1204.

[44] AMIN K, ROSTAMIZADEH A, SYED U. Repeated contextual auctions with strategic buyers[C]//Proceedings of the 27th International Conference on Neural Information Processing Systems. MIT Press, 2014: 622–630.

[45] COHEN M C, LOBEL I, LEME R P. Feature-based dynamic pricing[C]// Proceedings of the 2016 ACM Conference on Economics and Computation. ACM, 2016: 817.

[46]　MAO J, LEME R P, SCHNEIDER J. Contextual pricing for Lipschitz buyers[C]//Proceedings of the 32nd International Conference on Neural Information Processing Systems. Curran Associates,Inc., 2018: 5648–5656.

[47]　MEDINA A M, VASSILVITSKII S. Revenue optimization with approximate bid predictions[C]//Proceedings of the 31st International Conference on Neural Information Processing Systems. CurranAssociates Inc., 2017: 1856–1864.

Chapter 5 Summary and Future Directions

We propose the AI-driven mechanism design framework to tackle the challenges faced by the standard mechanism design theory. The framework combines tools and techniques from both domains.

We examine several mechanism design problems where standard theoretical approaches fail to give desirable solutions. In multi-dimensional mechanism design, we make use of the menu interpretation in economics and use neural networks to optimize a menu (see Chapter 2). The framework contains two networks: a mechanism network and a buyer network. The mechanism network produces a mechanism in the format of a menu. And the buyer network simply chooses the best menu item for him. We allow the buyer network to be either hard-coded according to a known utility function, or a network learned from buyer action data. Our approach not only can reproduce some known results but also can obtain optimal mechanisms that are unknown before. The menu interpretation guarantees that the resulting mechanism is both IC and IR.

In dynamic mechanism design, we show how the AI-driven mechanism design framework can be applied to both theories and applications (see Chapter 3). In Section 3.1, we aim to design the cost-per-action auction, where the advertiser pays after the user makes a purchase on his website. Furthermore, we need to guarantee that the mechanism is ex-post IR. Both these two properties clear the buyer's uncertainty. To prevent the buyer from lying about the user's actual actions on his website, we propose the "credit" mechanism, which is inspired by multi-armed bandit algorithms. Our mechanism gives a simple economic interpretation that can be easily implemented and guarantees IC with high probability. In Section 3.2, we aim to design a dynamic pricing policy for Baidu. We first propose an RNN-based buyer behavior model and fit the model with Baidu's enormous amount of data. Then we formulate the dynamic pricing problem as a Markov decision process and solve it using reinforcement learning algorithms. This framework has already been adopted by Baidu to increase revenue[1].

In multi-objective mechanism design, we use AI approaches to design mechanisms that optimize multiple objectives simultaneously (see Chapter 4). In Section 4.1, we study a parameterized mechanism that can tradeoff between revenue and social welfare. The tradeoff is easy to tune in the sense that both revenue and social welfare are monotones with respect to the mechanism parameter. Meanwhile, we show that such a mechanism always guarantees at least half the revenue of the optimal mechanism, regardless of the parameter. In Section 4.2, we use machine learning methods to learn a reasonable price for online ad auctions. We derive a new loss function from the concept of market clearing. Due to the convexity of the loss function, our method can easily converge to the global optimal point. Also, our experiments show that our method Pareto-dominates previous ones.

Although we have shown the effectiveness of our framework, there is still much to explore. For example, in Chapter 2, we apply the framework to the multi-item, single-buyer setting. How can we extend to the multiple buyer case, where the buyers cannot be represented by a single network? In this case, the menu provided to each buyer becomes a function of the value profile of other buyers. And the generated mechanism may cause feasibility problems if multiple buyers want the same item.

In Section 3.2, we simulate different pricing policies until convergence. It would be interesting to investigate whether the platform reached an equilibrium defined by the buyers' multi-dimensional preferences, and whether our framework has the ability of leading the agents to an equilibrium in such a complex environment.

In Section 4.2, we show that our approach can tradeoff between the match rate and revenue. It would be interesting if we can find the loss function that is Pareto-optimal in theory, in the sense that it Pareto-dominates all other possible loss functions. Similarly, can we do the same to tradeoff between other objectives?

Since the mechanism design problem can be viewed as a special Stackelberg game[2], one possible future research direction would be to extend the framework to the Stackelberg literature, where the abstract agent model and mechanism model become the leader model and the follower model, and study both theoretical and practical solutions within both one-shot and repeated context.

References

[1] Baidu Inc. Baidu Inc., first quarter 2018 financial reports [R/OL]. http://ir.baidu.com/static-files/626b8f84-5d34-49b7-b4ab-4f9f03cb8a2b.

[2] STACKELBERG H V. Market structure and equilibrium[J]. Springer Science & Business Media, 2010.